kevin m^ccloud

choosing colors

An expert choice of the best colors to use in your home

Watson-Guptill Publications
New York

Color accuracy and the limitations of this book
This volume has been printed in Hexachrome®, an advanced printing process that uses six component colors rather than the conventional four. While Hexachrome® offers over 3,000 controllable colors, there are still some limitations and variations within the printing process. As a result it is impossible to guarantee the fidelity of the colors reproduced.

The paint matches given in the four-page pull-out section have been matched to all the printed swatches in this book using paint manufacturers' color cards. However, neither the author nor the publisher can take responsibility for any discrepancies in color between a swatch color in this book and its corresponding specified manufacturers' color.

It is important to note that different batches of paint from any manufacturer will vary minutely in color. When buying paint, always check the batch numbers on the can and buy from the same batch whenever possible. If it is not possible to buy from the same batch, mix the cans to achieve a uniform color.

Editorial Director Anne Furniss
Creative Director Helen Lewis
Project Editor Lisa Pendreigh
Design Assistants Jim Smith and Katy Davis
Picture Researcher Nadine Bazar and Claire Limpus
Production Director Vincent Smith
Production Controllers Beverley Richardson

First published in the United States in 2003 by
Watson-Guptill Publications
a division of VNU Business Media, Inc.
770 Broadway, New York, New York 10003
www.watsonguptill.com

Text and palettes © Kevin McCloud 2003
Design and layout © Quadrille Publishing Ltd 2003

Library of Congress Control Number: 2003105409

ISBN 0-8230-0646-8

Manufactured in China

4 5 6 7 / 07 06 05

contents

WHY I WROTE THIS BOOK

I wanted to do just one thing with this book: provide a well-researched reference work that would be a useful working tool for the designer, decorator, homeowner, student, architect, craftsperson, artist, and anybody who gets fired up by the emotional power of color.

Having compiled this collection of color palettes, I'm now aware of how impossible it is to be universal. To include every historical or regional palette or every color model or every example of a "balanced" color scheme, if such things even exist, would demand an encyclopedic set of books, which nobody would then read. In fact those books that try to order color into harmonious symmetries of complementaries and split the color wheel into arrangements by fraction are very worthy, but also very dull.

Instead I've tried to convey collections of colors that best exemplify their time or place and that are powerful. A powerful palette to my mind is a palette that's not just a set of interesting or strong colors: it's something that has its own identity above those colors and that can trigger strong associations, sometimes in our subconscious, of a time or place or emotion. A single color can of course trigger such associations by itself, like a Miles Davis solo can. The palette, on the other hand, can work like a full orchestra.

There are colors and palettes in this book that may not please some people. There are no doubt some colors that are inaccurate, and I'm always grateful for corrections and additions. I have tried in every case to be as scholarly as possible in matching, cross-matching, and checking colors; but I do not claim that this book is an art history reference work: the palettes and colors are, ultimately, my choices. If anything, they are abstract representations, removed from the objects or events from which they are taken. They are distillations of time, of place, and of the ideas behind things. I hope you enjoy looking at them and using them.

HOW THIS BOOK WORKS

There are some 700 colors here arranged into 64 palettes. Although some palettes run over more than two pages, whenever you open a page in this book, the colors you see will form a coherent arrangement.

I could simply have provided a list of 700 interesting colors, but that would have been pointless. The choice of any color must be an informed one. We use color in an informed way, exploiting its perceived value and associations to convey unspoken and unwritten ideas, and emotions. So, every color in this book comes from somewhere, is connected to a thing or place or time, and is indicated as such, allowing you to make the most of its associated values if you want to.

What is even more powerful is the ability of a group of colors to convey a message, either very directly or in a more subtle and complex way, which is why nearly every color in this book is shown as part of a group of colors, a palette.

The palettes take their inspiration from all sorts of sources. Some are accurate reproductions of the colors of decorated objects: historic tiles from the Middle East; Sèvres porcelain from eighteenth-century France; Roman mosaics; Greek pottery—all objects of great value in the history of decoration and design. Others are taken from historical examples of wall paintings, whether it be Minoan or houses of the eighteenth century. Some are derived from the colors of place and country. Others are contemporary in origin, taking as their sources modern signage, the car, and new theoretical color systems.

You can extract colors from this book in a variety of ways: by copying an entire palette and employing the full force of any association or subtle value it may have; by drawing on a smaller group of colors; or by using just one color. In fact, the palettes are arranged in different ways too. Some are coherent wholes; others are split into distinct subgroups of a few colors.

Some of the palettes in this book are not assembled from one source or with any great plan behind them. They are simply collections of good colors from which you can choose at random. All the historical wall colors from the eighteenth, nineteenth, and early twentieth centuries are good examples of this kind of palette, from which you can simply choose a reasonably authentic color to paint your 1780s living room or your 1920s front door. If you do not feel constrained by the need for a period atmosphere, consult the sixteen-palette section "Pure Colors" (see pages 12–45). The palettes are just that: colors that I have chosen from among the 3,000 controllable colors in the six-color Hexachrome® printing process (see page 11) and that I have grouped by hue (blue, yellow-orange, etc.). These selections are not comprehensive by any means, but each color has its own separate and worthwhile character.

The palettes are not named according to their sources but according to their overall perceived character. This provides the hidden advantage of removing any prejudice you might have about a color or arrangement of colors. You could be very drawn to a set of colors for, say, your living room, or a project, or an ad campaign you are running. Were that palette to occur in a section marked "Wall Colors" and be called "Early Jericho", you might be put off from using it even before you had finished reading the title. Better to thumb through the book and just mark the palettes that catch your eye than be bogged down and prejudiced by words.

HOW TO FIND A PAINT COLOR

A supplementary list is provided at the end of this book with which you can find a commercial paint color to match any color shown here. Each color swatch in this book has a reference: the palette number, followed by the color number. For each of these I have given one commercial paint reference from Glidden, Benjamin Moore, Pratt and Lambert, or Sherwin Williams.

A NOTE ON THE COLOR REPRODUCTION

National and international standard colors have been matched by the comparison of Hexachrome® color swatches with approved control references (for example, the color-control atlases of the Natural Color System®, or NCS®, and the International Organization for Standardization, or ISO, references) and cross-matched with accompanying published *Munsell Books of Color*, Lab, or NCS® color references. See color model 4 on page 11 for a fuller understanding of the Hexachrome® printing process used to produce this book.

HOW COLOR WORKS

The following four pages contain various color models—structures that are used to explain how colors relate to each other and how we perceive them—that are all useful in helping to understand how the palettes in this book work.

Color models have been in use for millenia; Aristotle developed the first Western scale of colors, which in turn influenced Newton's decision to settle on seven colors for the rainbow (he had at various points thought there to be five or eleven). Even modern systems still refer to color in essentially Newtonian terms.

To an extent all color models are valid in some way. Even the most sophisticated 3-D color models in use by scientists still cannot account for some colors, so no one model necessarily reigns supreme; they are all fallible. That's because human vision itself is not consistent and it is not neat. It's not consistent because we, each of us, are blessed with minutely different configurations of optical receptors in our eyes (the rods and cones). It's not neat because vision is not a logical but a biological mechanism that has developed as an important tool for a myriad number of human activities: it is analogue, not digital, and its sensitivity to the colors of the rainbow varies (see color model 3 on page 10).

COLOR MODEL 1 IS THE ONE THAT WE LEARNED IN SCHOOL. THE PRIMARY PAINT COLORS—WHICH CANNOT BE PRODUCED BY MIXING OTHER COLORS—ARE YELLOW, RED, AND BLUE, AND THEIR SECONDARIES ARE MADE BY INTERMIXING. THE RESULT IS THAT WHEN THE MODEL IS ARRANGED AS A CIRCLE, THE COMPLEMENTARY OF RED IS GREEN (BEING OPPOSITE). COMPLEMENTARIES APPEAR TO "FIGHT" WHEN PLACED TOGETHER AND WHEN MIXED TOGETHER MAKE BROWN OF SOME KIND. MANY OF THE SUBTLER AND MORE COMPLEX COLORS IN THE PALETTES INVOLVE THE DILUTION OF ONE COLOR WITH A SMALL QUANTITY OF ITS COMPLEMENTARY PLUS THE ADDITION OF WHITE AND/OR BLACK. OTHER PALETTES PAIR COMPLEMENTARY COLORS TOGETHER TO DELIBERATE EFFECT. THIS MODEL IS A PRAGMATIC ONE BECAUSE IT WORKS FOR PIGMENTS AND CHEMICAL COLORANTS THAT IN TURN ARE OFTEN IMPERFECT. IT IS ALSO KNOWN AS THE "SUBTRACTIVE" MODEL BECAUSE AS THE COLORS ARE MIXED, THEY CANCEL OUT A DEGREE OF THEIR OWN LUMINOSITY AND BECOME DARKER. SO PURPLE AND GREEN ARE LESS BRIGHT THAN THEIR COMBINED CONSTITUENT PRIMARIES—A CASE OF THE SUM BEING LESS THAN THE PARTS.

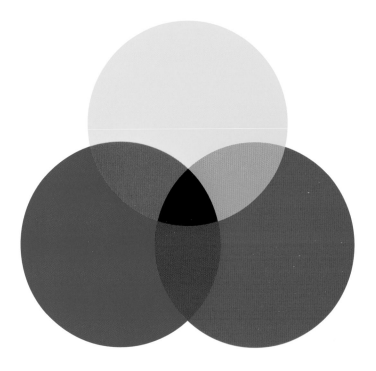

COLOR MODEL 2 IS A FOUR-COLOR PRIMARY MODEL, UNUSUAL AT FIRST SIGHT BUT ACTUALLY FORMULATED AS LONG AGO AS 1878 BY THE GERMAN PHYSIOLOGIST EWALD HERING, WHO THOUGHT THAT YELLOW, RED, BLUE, AND GREEN, TOGETHER WITH BLACK AND WHITE, FORMED A PALETTE OF SIX "NATURAL" COLORS. THIS IS PARTLY BECAUSE GREEN IS PERCEIVED AS A COLOR INDEPENDENT OF ITS COMPONENT SUBTRACTIVE COLORS, BLUE AND YELLOW. (THE EYE'S PHYSIOLOGY SETS UP THREE SIGNAL CHANNELS TO THE BRAIN, EACH ONE OF OPPOSING COLORS: BLACK-WHITE, RED-GREEN, BLUE-YELLOW. GREEN HAS ITS NAME UP THERE WITH THE OTHERS.)

THIS FOUR-COLOR PALETTE CREATES AN INTERESTING SET OF FOUR SECONDARY COLORS: ORANGE, VIOLET, TURQUOISE, AND LIME GREEN. ONE RESULT OF THIS, FOR EXAMPLE, IS THAT THE COMPLEMENTARY OF TURQUOISE BECOMES ORANGE, AND YOU CAN SEE A MUTED EXAMPLE OF THIS COMPLEMENTARY RELATIONSHIP IN PALETTE 58. THE FOUR-COLOR MODEL WAS REFINED IN THE TWENTIETH CENTURY, PUBLISHED AND REPUBLISHED, AND THEN TECHNICALLY PERFECTED BY THE SWEDISH COLOR CENTER FOUNDATION, WHICH ISSUED IT AS THE STANDARD COLOR ATLAS OF THE NATURAL COLOR SYSTEM (NCS) IN 1979. IT'S NOW ADOPTED AS SEVERAL NATIONAL STANDARDS AND BY PAINT AND COATINGS MANUFACTURERS WORLDWIDE. PALETTE 62 CONTAINS ALL THE PRIMARY, SECONDARY, AND TERTIARY (BETWEEN THE SECONDARIES) COLORS OF THIS FOUR-COLOR SYSTEM.

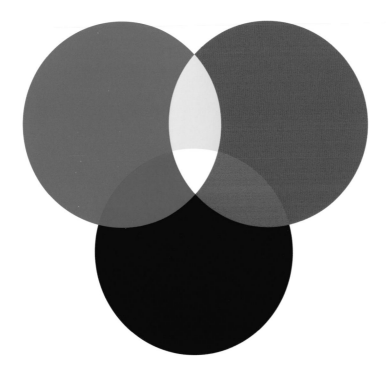

COLOR MODEL 3 REVERTS TO THREE PRIMARIES, AND THEY'RE DIFFERENT AGAIN FROM COLOR MODEL 1. THE REASON IS THAT THESE ARE THE PRIMARY AND SECONDARY COLORS OF LIGHT: GREEN, WARM RED, AND PURPLE-BLUE LIGHT WHEN MIXED TOGETHER PRODUCE WHITE LIGHT (JUST AS RED, YELLOW, AND BLUE PAINT ARE SUPPOSED TO MAKE BLACK BUT, BECAUSE OF PIGMENT IMPERFECTION, MAKE A MURKY BROWN). THEIR SECONDARY COLORS ARE ALSO INTERESTING: CYAN BLUE (SIMILAR TO TURQUOISE), MAGENTA, AND YELLOW, WHICH MOST BIZARRELY OF ALL IS PRODUCED BY MIXING RED AND GREEN LIGHT. NOTE THAT BECAUSE THE SECONDARIES RESULT FROM THE ADDITION OF TWO OTHER LIGHT COLORS, THEY ARE ALSO MORE LUMINOUS. NOT SURPRISINGLY, THIS IS CALLED AN ADDITIVE PALETTE.

THERE IS NO MAGIC BEHIND THE CHOICE OF COLORS AND NO ALCHEMY IN THEIR MIXING. THE CHOICE OF RED, GREEN, AND BLUE PRIMARIES FROM AMONG THE COLORS OF THE VISIBLE SPECTRUM (I.E. THE RAINBOW) ALL COMES DOWN TO THE WAY WE'RE BUILT. WE PERCEIVE A VERY NARROW BAND OF ELECTROMAGNETIC RADIATION (WHICH INCLUDES RADIO AND GAMMA WAVES) AND WE CALL THAT VISIBLE PORTION LIGHT. THE THREE TYPES OF SENSORS ON OUR RETINAS THAT RESPOND TO DIFFERENT COLORS WITHIN THE VISIBLE SPECTRUM HAVE PEAK SENSITIVITY IN DIFFERENT AREAS: ONE PEAKS IN THE BLUE PART OF THE SPECTRUM, ONE IN THE GREEN, AND ONE IN THE RED. IF WE HAD SENSORS THAT WERE SENSITIVE TO INFRARED OR ULTRAVIOLET (AS SOME ANIMALS DO), WE MIGHT SEE MORE COLORS. AS IT IS, BECAUSE WE HAVE ONLY THREE TYPES (PLUS ONE FOR MONOCHROME VISION), OUR ENTIRE COLOR WORLD IS DEPENDENT ON THEM: ALL PERCEIVABLE COLORS ARE MADE UP FROM VARIOUS COMBINATIONS OF THEIR ACTIVITIES. THAT GIVES US A MEASLY, SEPARATELY IDENTIFIABLE SIXTEEN MILLION COLORS TO PLAY WITH.

COLOR MODEL 4 TAKES THE SECONDARY COLORS OF LIGHT—CYAN, MAGENTA, AND YELLOW—AND WORKS THEM BACKWARD. THE THEORY IS THAT IF YOU TAKE THREE SHEETS OF TRANSPARENT PLASTIC IN THESE THREE COLORS, YOU SHOULD BE ABLE TO PRODUCE THE LIGHT PRIMARIES BY SUBTRACTION. THUS A SHEET OF CYAN PLASTIC FILM HELD OVER A SHEET OF MAGENTA PLASTIC FILM SHOULD GIVE A LESS LUMINOUS, BUT BLUE LIGHT. IT WORKS A LITTLE LIKE MIXING PAINT, AND THESE THEORETICAL SUBTRACTIVE PRIMARIES—CYAN, MAGENTA, AND YELLOW—OUGHT (IN OPPOSITION TO COLOR MODEL 3) TO MAKE BLACK WHEN OVERLAID. OF COURSE THEY DON'T BECAUSE COLORED PLASTIC, LIKE COLORED ANYTHING (OTHER THAN LIGHT), IS NEVER 100 PERCENT TOTALLY PURELY COLORED.

IT'S THE SAME STORY WITH PRINTING INKS. THIS MODEL LIES BEHIND MODERN PRINTING METHODS, WHICH USE CYAN, MAGENTA, AND YELLOW TRANSPARENT INKS OVER WHITE PAPER (A SOURCE OF REFLECTED LIGHT) TO REPRODUCE FULL-COLOR PHOTOGRAPHS IN BOOKS AND MAGAZINES. IN PRACTICE, PRINTERS ALSO USE BLACK TO BOLSTER THE PERFORMANCE OF THE THREE COLORS, AND THE RESULTING PRINTING METHOD (WHICH IS PART-ADDITIVE, PART-SUBTRACTIVE) IS KNOWN AS CMYK PROCESS PRINTING, NOW USED WORLDWIDE.

BUT CMYK HAS ALWAYS HAD ITS WEAKNESSES, NOTABLY POOR GREENS AND ESPECIALLY ORANGES, WHICH ALWAYS LOOK DULL AND MUDDY, MAINLY DUE, AGAIN, TO THE TECHNICAL LIMITATIONS OF THE INKS. PANTONE®, ONE OF THE LARGEST COLOR AUTHORITIES IN THE WORLD AND CERTAINLY THE SINGLE MOST PERSUASIVE VOICE IN THE GRAPHICS AND PRINTING INDUSTRIES, HAS SOLVED THESE PROBLEMS TO A LARGE EXTENT WITH THE INTRODUCTION OF TWO FURTHER INK COLORS, GREEN AND ORANGE, AS SHOWN ON THE LEFT. TOGETHER WITH CMYK THEY MAKE A SIX-COLOR PROCESS METHOD CALLED HEXACHROME®. THIS BOOK IS ONE OF VERY FEW CONSUMER VOLUMES TO BE PRINTED IN HEXACHROME®; IT WAS AN ESSENTIAL CHOICE FOR THE ACCURATE COLOR RENDERING OF THE PALETTES AND AN ADDED ADVANTAGE IN THAT IT REPRODUCES VIBRANT PHOTOGRAPHS WELL.

pure colors

Starting on this page are sixteen groups of colors that sequentially follow each other around the color wheel, starting here with yellow. These are consciously subjective selections: in other words colors I like, chosen for their interest, importance, or "useability". It's by no means a comprehensive range; that would require an encyclopedic volume!

The "color" palettes are followed by a palette of grays, one of browns, and one of pale neutral colors. The layout of the colors is self-explanatory although I have used an unconventional range of hues (see notes to this section in "Notes to the Palettes" on page 176). The palettes can be divided into subgroups. You might find that all the colors in one column or row have a family character that can be exploited by using them altogether.

1 A rich chrome/cadmium yellow of pure hue. Similar to Chinese yellow—the color of Imperial Chinese robes of all periods. Use with care: this color advances and together with black suggests danger.

2 A good bright mustardy ochre. Very useable, especially with the other colors in this column.

3 A clear, cool yellow with a trace of warmth about it. A color much used on textiles during the First and Second French Empire and a typical yellow of Dresden (Meissen) porcelain.

4 If this yellow were any deeper it might cloy. As it is, this warm, sunny tint is approachable and unthreatening. Another yellow found in Chinese robes of all periods. Also similar to Alessandro Mendini's "Giallo Atelier" and Norman Foster's choice for applied color at the Commerzbank headquarters in Germany.

5 Cool, pale primrose yellow. Use with care since this color can easily appear green under the wrong light.

6 A deeper and slightly greener version of color 5. Use these two colors with any from the bottom row in this palette. Another Dresden tint.

7 Paler than color 9, a pretty and luminous, slightly greenish yellow, the color of emergent foliage. Use with colors below and to the left.

8 This warm buttery—almost orange—cream is the color of a good yellow ochre tint, or more accurately a Naples yellow tint. As such it is unlikely ever to appear greenish under blue-biased daylight, such as that from a north-facing window or from under an overcast sky.

9 Adding a small quantity of black to yellow immediately turns it greenish. Adding gray produces approachable 1950s-looking tones such as this. Use with any of the colors immediately surrounding it.

10 This is an interestingly ambiguous color: gray-brown-yellow-green-buff. This combination of personalities must mean that it's versatile and useable.

11 Almost gray, a delicate and very unusual tint worth experimenting with, particularly with colors 10 and 12.

12 A pale cream that is neutral but with a slightly weird greenish echo: the color that the moon sometimes takes on. Hence Alessandro Mendini's name for it: "Giallo Lunare".

1 The kind of deep warm yellow that's tolerable to live with and the color of the finest yellow ochre.

2 The color of Indian yellow. Bright, clear, and warm with none of the cloying quality of color 3.

3 This rich color is used more or less internationally as a prosaic safety color (at construction plants, etc). Useful to suggest this idea.

4 The color of lead-tin yellow, a prized synthetic medieval pigment. Deep and more complex than color 3. Appropriate as an architectural color.

5 A deep ochre with brown in it. Complex, with "depth" and used underneath gilding.

6 A tint of raw sienna, a beautifully warm manila/ beige that's a very useable decorating color,

especially with pale cream (e.g. color 16) and as a warm, dusty antiquing color.

7 A very 1950s yellow, warm and dense. Look at it with only the colors below and the three to the left.

8 The color of ripe pineapples, a cheering tint that needs the duller colors on this page. Works best with the yellows in the fourth column on the opposite page.

9 A sludge color, orange-yellow-green-brown. An excellent foil to all the intense yellows of the top row.

10 A warmer tint of the color above it that is a more versatile decorating color. Suggestive of sand or pale hide. Good with all the colors on the bottom row.

11 A vibrant, dense, thick, buttery yellow, a tint of chrome yellow or the color of Naples yellow.

12 Orange squash in a glass, and so I suppose a refreshing color. Use as part of a palette comprising only the lower eight of these colors.

13 Manila or antique buff, a versatile decorating color that is an orange-tinged raw sienna tint. Complex and especially good with other colors in this row and the intense color above it.

14 An ochre tint with a hint of lemon: the perfect partner for orange squash (color 12). Try also with color 6 and, on the opposite page, colors 2 and 4.

15 Sweeter and less muddy than color 14. A versatile ochre tint that refuses to appear green, even under the most glowering of cloudy skies.

16 A paler tint of color 15 with all the same properties but greater reflectance.

03 orange

1 Burnt orange, almost tan. Use as an earthy detail color with any other color on this page.

2 Bright and warm, the color of orange squash. Try it as a detail color with all of the colors in this column.

3 Mid-orange hue. Intense and pure.

4 Deep, rich, and moving toward red, this is a deeper realgar color, a valued pigment in use in ancient times.

5 The color of orange lacquer, with a brownish bias. A useable key or detail color with all the colors in this row or below. (Obscure the top row to see how this works.)

6 A warm umber brown that actually contains a lot of orange. Very useful because it moves toward a more neutral position and is good with all the colors in the lower half of this palette and many of those paler ones opposite.

7 A good leather color and a good earth color, being that of raw sienna pigment. Look at it with just colors 6, 10, and 11.

8 Clean and well-scrubbed flesh pink, slightly brown and very useful.

9 A good "natural" leather color. Use it with the color next to it and the other "earthier" colors here.

10 A slight tint of dirty yellow ochre or raw sienna. A very complex, useable color. Use with the colors above and below, and with colors 8 and 11 opposite.

11 It looks reddish but it's made primarily with orange and black inks on this page. This is a very warm earth color that can support a lot of the other, less useable colors on this page.

12 Rosy flesh color. Use it with stronger colors if you want to avoid these connotations of the 1970s.

13 A less intense version of the color above, with more yellow in it. Use as a key color with others in this row, and with color 10 or 11.

14 Variously labeled light donkey or mushroom, a popular cool beige-gray used as a decorating color.

15 Is this beige? I don't know. This color is still quite intense. Use carefully or choose a lighter version. Good with the other colors in this column.

16 A really delicate mix of orange and pale gray. Use with colors from the neutral or brown palettes.

1 The color of red lead pigment that since the fourteenth century has been known as Saturn red.

2 A pinker version of color 1, a near-hue with a similarly dusty quality and equivalent to modern red lead pigment. Use these colors with the brownish reds below.

3 This is a color of many meanings, being that of a version of the ancient pigment vermilion. Much used in Western art and decorative painting and warmer than in its Chinese incarnation.

4 A warm brown made with plenty of orange-red. The color of good-quality hematite (iron oxide) pigment.

5 Pale orange buff or flesh tone without any glaring orange glow. Use with any of the colors below.

6 A cross between brick red and burnt orange. Intense, advancing, warm, and uncompromising.

7 A more approachable and muddied version of color 6, the meeting point of hematite, red lead, and vermilion pigments. Similar to BCC "Brick Red|". Useful for decoration.

8 A pretty "bruised pink" color that is soft and purplish. Very useable as an indoor paint color and one that I've used a lot.

9, 10, 11, and 12 These red oxide tints are all useable, intense colors, each with a different character. Color 9 is orange-biased, color 10 is cooler and more purplish. Color 11 is pinker, a tint of Mars orange. Color 12 is a lighter tint of color 9. Roughly they are tonally equivalent and collectively form a base range of colors to which any other on this page can be added.

13 This pale plastic pink belongs in an Art Deco interior or on a neoclassical ceiling. It's a tint of red lead. Moderate it with any of the murkier colors opposite. A vibrant color.

14 A tint of color 8 that is just as useable with an even more pronounced purplish leaning. Good with off-white or any of the colors in the row above.

15 A complex pale pinky-beige—or warm pale brown. Can be used with off-white, but really comes into its own as a toning color that can be used to moderate any other color on this page or that opposite.

16 Another Art Deco and neoclassical color that looks particularly good with olive greens, the murkier colors opposite, any color in this column, and/or color 15.

1 Bright mid-red hue, equivalent to "Signal Red", scarlet, or pure mid-hue vermilion pigment.

2 This printed swatch uses the same inks in the same quantity as color 1 but with the addition of a black.

3 A dusty, slightly pink-red. Useful as a decorating color and redolent of the color of Oriental lacquer.

4 Adding black to red produces rich browns, which can be modified by adding orange, yellow, or green. This is a very useable color.

5 A striking intense tint of color 1. Slightly synthetic in quality but unusual and arresting.

6 An interesting brown. In the right light it can be described almost as red—or even as brown-pink. Dusty with a plum-colored undertone. Very useable.

7 A dusty crimson with a slightly pink character.

8 A tone of color 7 made more complex by the addition of brown and gray. Note that the four colors on the top right of this page all make a family.

9 An even lighter tint of color 1. Cooler than its hue, but with the same strawberry character as that above.

10 Another intense dusty pink-brown that sits in between the colors above and beneath it: next to it color 6 appears a straight brown while color 14 looks innocently pink. Compare these two colors to others around them without referring to color 10.

11 A tint of another porcelain color, "Delft Rose". Use with other colors in this column.

12 A dense and somber tone of the bluish reds on

this side of the page. A key moderating color to use with the stronger pinks and reds. Complex and useful.

13 Its reddish tinge makes this a key moderating color for this palette, in particular for this column and in combination with other colors on this page, where it will look beige. However, it appears almost pink when viewed in isolation, so use with care.

14 A pink the color of red dusty earth and a key color in this column of four. Again, it looks very different when viewed in isolation.

15 A more intense and slightly less innocent pink than color 9, also slightly cooler. Very good when used together with the other three colors in this row.

16 A cleaner and even more bluish tint of color 12 that is very useable.

1 Warm reddish magenta, the color of the brightest cloths dyed with madder root and similar to rose madder pigment. Also known as "Carmine" and as "Carmin Cramoisi" (Repertoire), and as "Tyrian Rose" (Ridgway) for its supposed likeness to the finer light colors produced by dyeing cloth with the purple dye from the murex shellfish. These names suggest a color that has been prized and sought after for centuries. It is an extraordinary color.

2 Often called "Pourpre de Tyr" (Repertoire) or "Tyrian Purple", this color is supposedly the deepest hue attainable from murex dye. It is also Pantone® "Rubine Red", a deep and powerful hue, half-purple, half-pink, and like its neighbors, bewitching.

3 Magenta (or fuchsine), the color of an aniline dye named after the Battle of Magenta in 1859 and as it appears as one of the three modern process colors used for printing in color. Unforgiving and totally uncompromising, as vivid a hue as you can expect to see. Use with extreme caution.

4 A complex deep purplish plum, a shade of color 2. Use in place of colors 1 and 3 with any other colors in the palette for much subtler combinations. Especially good with colors in the two right-hand columns of this palette.

5 Another shade of color 2, colder and harder. Soften it with any color in the right half of this page.

6 Mauve, and not the delicate (actually faded) tint that we think of but the color of the brilliant dye invented in 1856 by William Henry Perkins. It was the first of the somewhat fugitive coaltar (aniline) dyes and was quickly adopted as the fashionable color for dress fabrics, giving rise to the "Mauve Decade". Overdue for revival.

7 A more plum-colored, blue-tinged version of color 5. A key color in this palette that can be used with any other in isolation or as part of a group.

8 Warm intense pink but with plenty of magenta in it. Actually a slightly shaded tint of color 1 with which it works well. Try it also as part of a group made up of colors from this column only.

9, 10, 11, 12, 13, 14, 15, and 16 These are a group of pinks of varying degrees of bluish coolness. Their collective character is of the 1930s and 1940s, and used together their differing characters are subdued under the general identity of one palette. Colors 11 and 12 are particularly complex and can be used well together, while color 14 is also quite subtle.

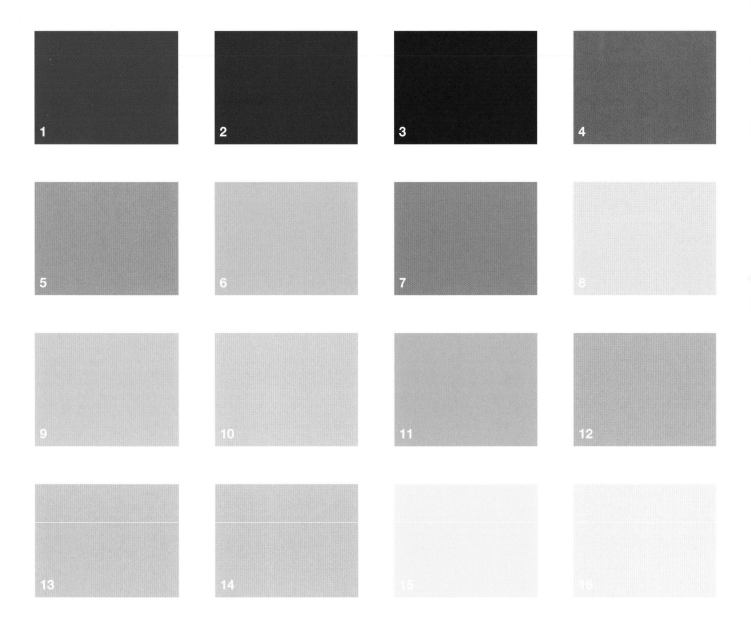

1 The color of cobalt violet pigment (cobalt phosphate) and a name in use since 1859. A vibrant purple infused with magenta that works with other colors in this row or those in this column.

2 Reddish purple, again a color that vibrates and is tinged with magenta. Use with any other color in this palette. The color of mineral, or manganese, violet.

3 Purple, if such a thing exists without any obvious blue or magenta content. Very close to spectrum violet. More particular than color 2 as to which color it likes to keep company with.

4 Purple often occurs in this book as a pivotal color in a palette, especially when muted with either gray or brown—or both. When shaded or toned in this way, purple can take on a brooding, bruised look but also an interesting, complex quality. This color

and color 12 illustrate just how pleasingly ambiguous purple can be.

5 Purple-gray: a name that is frankly off-putting but a color that is not. Intense and useable, especially in complex palettes of many colors.

6 Deep lilac, uncomplicated and direct. Use it with any combination of colors from this row and below.

7 An attractive bluish purple tint that hovers between being intense and dusty. A tint of a color associated for several centuries with the dauphin of France.

8, 9, and 10 All lilac tints of varying degrees of purity. Color 10 is the most complex.

11 Deep lavender blue, a color right on the cusp of purple and blue and one that will

consequently change character according to prevailing lighting conditions.

12 A cool neutral that is very useable on its own but also with any other color here. Subtle.

13 Another lilac color, slightly bluer than color 10 and more complex.

14 Even more gray than color 13. A good and unusual decorating color and another useful half-neutral color that will work with any other on this page.

15 Powdery lavender blue-violet.

16 Palest gray-lilac. Try it as part of just this column of colors, or as part of just this row, or as part of just the lower half of this palette.

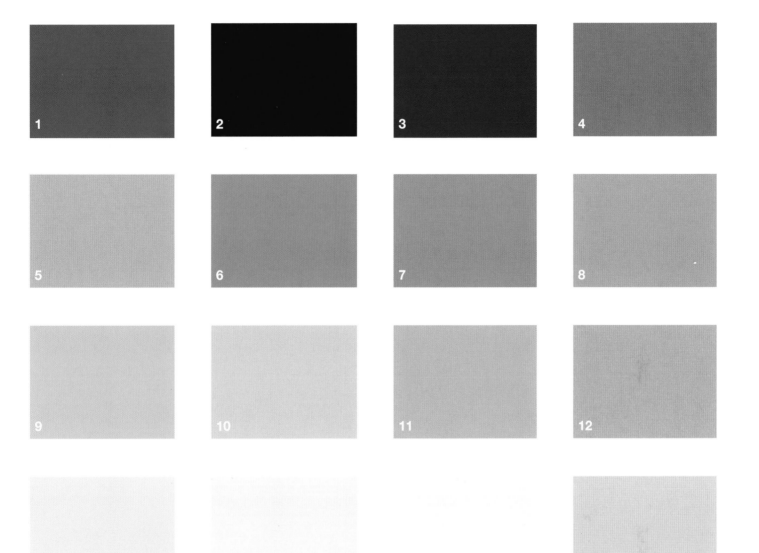

1 A good clean and bright red-tinged violet, a color that appears vivid under sunlight and heavy and brooding indoors.

2 Deeper than color 1, the color of ultramarine blue pigment. A color of great depth and purity.

3 A lighter and less purple ultramarine hue, closer to the architectural detail color used in Greece, etc.

4 A color of indigo-dyed cotton. An intense but useable and almost hypnotic tone of violet-blue. Use as a key color with any other here, particularly colors from this row and below.

5 Warm, grayed violet. The color to use indoors if color 1 appeals. All the colors in this and the lower rows on both pages have been partly chosen for their "aerial" qualities (i.e. their suggestiveness of sky or air).

6 A warm pretty tint of a reddish ultramarine blue. An intense color, the zenith of an evening blue sky.

7 A more assertive and vibrant version of color 8 with more of the interest of color 4.

8 Another indigo or woad color.

9 A tint of color 5. Less brooding and complex, and a little perkier.

10 A more useable tint of the color above it, complex and warm. Perhaps the most versatile color here.

11 A tint of color 7 with plenty of airy depth to it. Sufficiently grayed to make it interesting.

12 This delicate grayish brown-purple and the color

below it almost belong in the next palette but for the fact they are slightly too warm. A useable decorating color that is very complex and satisfying to look at.

13 This color connects back to purple. It's a clever mix of gray and bluish violet that evidently makes a successful architectural color since Norman Foster chose it for his Research Center in Stamford, England.

14 A pretty powdery tint of the color above. Like color 10, it is saved from daintiness by the gray.

15 About as pale (and still warm-looking) as blue can go without appearing gray. A pretty color but with a bit of sobriety.

16 Bluish pale lilac with a cool atmospheric "aerial" quality. Delicate and sophisticated.

1 A deep, velvety, and powerful blue, invasive indoors but an assertive and fashionable color outdoors.

2 A color of cobalt blue pigment, mid-blue with no bias to red or green. A magical and underused hue of great purity, redolent of the deepest summer skies.

3 A slight shade of color 2, cooler and less strident.

4 This blue is deeply shaded, restrained, and a little ambiguous. It finds a lot of exterior uses as a sort of "soft black": it's therefore good on front doors. Try it against the cooler colors on the opposite page.

5 An intense milky tint. Red-tinged, this color neither advances nor recedes but hovers atmospherically.

6 A pure cobalt tint, as refreshing as its hue above but more useable and more suggestive of the sky's

zenith. Try it with all or some of the colors below.

7 This blue veers toward cyan: it is cool and powerful. Fresh and bright when used as a detail color with others in this column.

8 A pale tint of the color above, this is a pleasing warm gray-blue that can be used as a background to any color on this page. A good decorating color.

9 An intense milky violet-blue that has a slightly cloying quality because unlike cooler pale blues, it does not appear to recede. A luxurious color.

10 A good deep sky blue with great optical depth. Suggestive of open space. Note how all the colors in this lower half of the page have an "aerial" quality.

11 Bright dusty mid-hue blue, a tint of cobalt and an

ingenuous and clean blue for it.

12 A tint of ultramarine blue. An exquisite decorating color with depth and character. Any color in this row has a good relationship with the violet-blues in the preceding palette.

13 Delicate, cool, and pale. Use with all of the other colors in this row.

14 Another innocent blue, but cleaner and much paler than color 11. Very elegant.

15 A smokier version of color 14 with a harder edge and so more complex. Good indoors.

16 Pale, grayed, and slightly violet, this blue is a good background color with any combination of colors from this column, this row, or the preceding palette.

1 This deep marine blue is a good foil for most of the colors on this page or with deep greens. The color of impure azurite.

2 This color is cyan, a modern printing color in full-color lithography and a vivid, uncompromising hue. That is because, like magenta and yellow, it is an optical secondary color, produced by the stimulation of two out of the eye's three groups of color receptors.

3 Deep porcelain blue, redolent of Middle Eastern and Oriental ceramics and more complex than color 2. Should be used more, especially outside.

4 Adding black to color 3 produces a harder, inky gasoline shade, last popular in the 1960s as a car color.

5 A cool blue-gray that, unlike the other tints on this page, has no green in it. Very versatile with colors on this page and opposite and with pale ochres and other earth colors.

6 Not an easy color to live with, but loud and clear. Surround it with other subtler blues, as here, to good effect.

7, 11, and 15 Here are three tinted tones of a delicate blue-green-gray: complex and ambiguous colors that will all subtly change character according to the prevailing lighting. They are cusp colors on the edge of blue/green that defy our color memory—the brain's powers of self-persuasion—and look different under direct sun, cloud, or tungsten lighting. Color 11 is cleaner and slightly more green.

8 This is a more acceptable and less sulky tint of color 4 above. Like the colors beneath, an interesting tone that can be used as a detail color with any of the colors in this row and below.

9 and 13 Two tints of a clean greenish blue that are very useable and important in "lifting" the character of the lower half of this palette. Color 13 is of unimpeachable delicacy: it is the color of my kitchen.

10 For a dirty tint, this color still hums. It looks like a ceramic color or something from the eighteenth century. Strong but useable.

12 and 16 The most watery, glasslike colors on this page. Color 16 is particularly useable for decoration, while color 12 is slightly harder and better suited as the controlling partner to color 8.

14 Pale duck egg blue. Delicate and slightly icy.

11 turquoise

1 Turquoise blue. Use as a detail color with any other on the left-hand side of the page.

2 As turquoise moves toward green so it appears darker. Use with any color from the lower three rows.

3 A hard bluish green. Use as a detail color against any of the bluer tints, left, to soften its synthetic quality.

4 A deep foliage color. Less synthetic than color 3. Like many of these colors, suggestive of the sea.

5 Gasoline blue, a grayed tone of turquoise, and more useable as a result, although lacking in immediacy. A powerful color with a brooding aquatic quality.

6 Jade. More useable and delicate than color 5, veering toward green. It has a dusty appearance, particularly when used with the colors in the top row.

7 Use this as the dominant color in a palette consisting of this row alone.

8 This deep and ambiguous blue-gray-green is a cusp color: it changes character under different lighting conditions. Use as the dominant color with others from this row.

9 A hard, cool, and slightly synthetic turquoise tint. A clean and invigorating color.

10 A pseudo-historical, slightly brownish tone that will work very well with any color on this page and "root" any mixture of them. A complex and deep color.

11 A delicate and subtle 1920s-flavored green with a clean mint color. Use with any of the colors in the right-hand column to invigorate them.

12 A tint of color 8 and more useable for it. Use as a core or dominant color with any of the others on this page. A cusp color.

13 A highly versatile and brown-tinged pale turquoise that is slightly ambiguous and soft in its effect. Use with any of the colors on the lower half of this page.

14 A tint of the color above, this is a delicate but not washed-out pale gray-blue with a hint of green. Ambiguous and a good partner for the color to its right and with any in the right-hand column.

15 A cooler mint green than color 7 and subtler too. Use with the right-hand column and the bottom row.

16 Subtle, washed-out, and atmospheric, this is the color of gray sea. When used with more intense colors, it will appear gray and hazy.

12 green

1 A slightly bluish emerald green with a synthetic quality. Use in small quantities with any color on the opposite page.

2 A pure and vivid hue green, corresponding to the pigment emerald green.

3 This deep green contains enough black to render it approachable. But it retains the vivacity of the hue.

4 Deep and toned, this bronze green is good outside. The color of terre verte or chrome oxide pigment.

5 The most complex color on this page, an almost sea green. Good with the two colors beneath.

6 A more vivid version of color 5, dense and appealing. Its bluish cast suggests an almost synthetic quality, yet it is the color of deepest verdigris.

7 A dusty tint of color 3, suggestive of grass. This is a useable, reasonably intense green that will accommodate other intense colors such as orange and red because of its gray content.

8 A light eau de nil, so named because the Nile's water is this color. Another restrained, milky color.

9 A color right on the edge of blue and green and so a cusp color that will respond to changes in light color. A key color for combining with any number of the paler examples on this page.

10 A good mid-verdigris color, bright and clear, suggestive of 1820s and 1920s Oriental interiors.

11 A pale and ambiguous bronze green with character. Another good decorating color, the color of a terre verte tint.

12 An extremely subtle milky tint that is almost gray. Understated and refined.

13 A chalky pale verdigris, bluish and toned with gray. This is a very useable color that is similar to many "historic" or "Scandinavian" greens. A cusp color.

14 A greener and lighter version of color 12. A subtle green-blue that works well on walls. A cusp color and a very flexible ground color for many other color combinations.

15 Delicate and slightly yellowish, a good 1920s pale pea pod color.

16 A warm green-gray (warm because of the small amount of yellow present). Very useable because of its depth and ambiguity.

1 This vivid hue is as clear and bright as green gets before it becomes obviously yellow-biased.

2 Another good grass or foliage green, particularly good with the paler colors, below right.

3 A clever way of using lime green is to moderate it by darkening—but not to the point where it turns dull. This shade is often employed in commercial fabric dyeing and printing because of its useability.

4 Moss color, or bright olive. Appears almost brown when placed with bright greens and so can be used to moderate a scheme that uses them.

5 This is an interesting color because it seems to be slightly veiled with blue—despite containing a large quantity of yellow. A key color when used with the surrounding brighter colors.

6 Hovering between lime green and green, this is the color of spring foliage. Use with all the colors surrounding it or more specifically with only the colors in this column.

7 This is lime green at pretty well its most intense (although fluorescing versions appear brighter). A popular decorating color during the late 1990s.

8 This is a tint of color 4 and is much more cheerful, complex, and useable. Use it with brighter greens such as colors 2, 3, and 7.

9 The bright color of wool dyed with woad (blue) and then overdyed with weld (yellow) to produce green.

10 A very useable and subtle green that retains some intensity. Use it as a key color among a palette of neutrals such as those below.

11 Almost creamy gray, this ambiguous green is a flexible decorating color. Use with off-white and any other colors from this muted section of the palette.

12 A light olive color with a real period feel. Use with the colors to the left and below.

13 A popular early twentieth-century color, another muddy tint that can be called eau de nil.

14 A very clear and assertive 1920s color. Use with the stronger colors, above and to the left and right, to control it.

15 Bluer version of color 14 and even more useable.

16 Greenish grays have a fresh but still antique character. They work best with "natural"-colored contemporary schemes.

14 gray

You may not think so, but gray is a very useful color, especially as an additive to other more intense shades. This is particularly true in decorating. Try mixing your own paint colors and you will inevitably, in the end, have to add a little gray, simply in order to render the color softer and more lively. This simulates adding some of a color's complementary, a time-honored artist's technique for livening up a color so that it appears less synthetic.

1, 5, 9, and 13 The four colors in the first column are made just by printing varying intensities of black ink. The grays they make obviously depend on the color of the paper used for this book, but generally these are neutral: neither warm nor cool. Mixing white with black pigment (especially vegetable carbon) produces bluish tints, so blue in fact that an eighteenth-century method for pale blue was to add vine black to white distemper. In comparison, color 13 looks positively warm, the kind of deep "Battleship Gray" adopted in World War I.

2 and 6 These are other tints of black, but color 6 has some blue in it. This smoky color was used by Sir Norman Foster to paint the Century Tower in Tokyo.

3, 7, 10, 11, 14, and 15 Colors 10 and 14 are both tinged with green, giving these grays an austere character, whereas colors 3, 7, 11, and 15 (the third column) are all colored with warm red. The resulting deep tone (color 15) is almost brown but with a suedy dustiness. Color 11 still looks brown, but the two tints (colors 3 and 7) have a truly ambiguous character: warm gray in some lights, fawn in others.

4, 8, 12, and 16 The final column contains brownish grays made with raw umber and white. Color 12 is perhaps the most beautiful color on this page and a versatile decorating color. Colors 4 and 8 are excellent off- and dirty whites for use in period decoration. Never underestimate how white these can appear when in the company of other more intense colors.

15 brown

If adding gray softens a color, adding brown renders it even more supple and muddy. Each brown has a bias: to red, green, orange, yellow. The most resolute colors are those with a red or green content. The most interesting are those with a joint orange and yellow bias.

1 Tan: half-brown and half-orange. Oriental in origin.

2 The purplish hue of deep red oxide.

3 A clear tint of burnt sienna. A beautiful deep plaster pink.

4 This purplish brown yields beautiful, ambiguous tints when mixed with white or gray. Even when this intense, it has a dusty subtlety.

5 An interesting brown: apparently cool, it is made with pink, orange, and some olive green. A clever mix.

6 The color of rich red ochre, a hue that will yield subtle strawberry pinks when mixed with white.

7 Use this warm "donkey" brown with color 5. Subtle and mature, it makes a good decorating color.

8 A tint of color 11, with more yellow in it. Another powerful but good decorating color.

9 A hot deep ochre or raw sienna.

10 A beautiful brick red.

11 Light raw umber, greenish and dry looking. Perhaps the most versatile brown for adding to other colors, for tinting white, and for use in glazes and waxes.

12 A pretty pale cocoa or chestnut, not unrelated to colors 5 and 7 with which it works very well.

13 A yellow-orange brown, like deep raw sienna. Good with orange and green.

14 Cooler than color 6, more like burnt sienna and so good with color 3. Another ancient pigment based on iron oxide.

15 Deep raw umber, very greenish and almost khaki green or olive.

16 Another complex brown, made with yellow and orange but with a cool cast. Powerful.

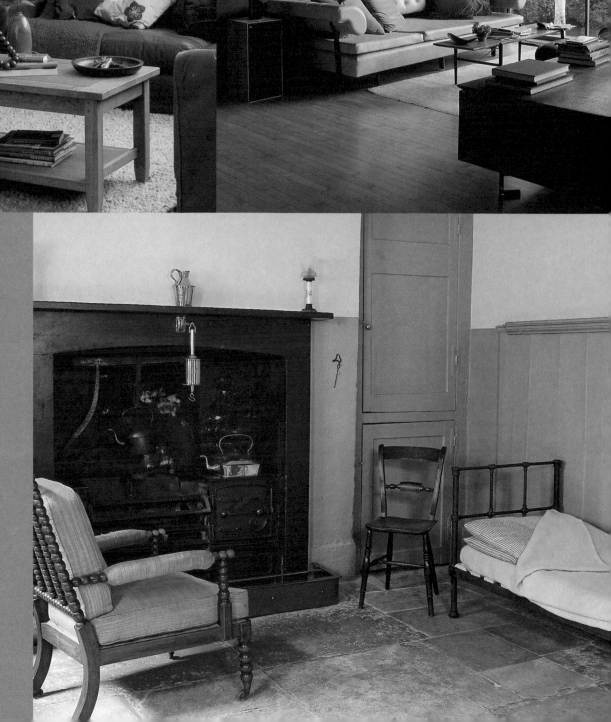

A palette of "neutrals" might strike you as irrelevant and already out of date, but in fact these colors are often the hardest colors to get right. The problem comes in producing a color that is truly neutral, and that depends on the right choice of pigments: ones that have a broad earthiness about them. Given that most interiors and other human environments are composed of a fair proportion of gray-brown shadow, and given that we light our spaces with predominantly warm light and that we furnish them with many natural warm-colored materials (stone, wood, skin, even cement), it follows that neutral colors in such a setting often need to be warm. This very useful palette represents mixes of ancient earth pigments such as raw and burnt umber, and raw sienna. The colors are indispensable.

1 This delicate pale beige is a good wall color. It's warm and parchment-like.

2 This deep and sandy beige is a complex warm color. Good for intimate spaces because it advances. Also good as a warm "antiquing" color when used as a wash or glaze on furniture.

3 A cooler color than 1, 2, or 4. An excellent warm off-white to use with deep or rich reds, and browns.

4 Mid-beige, halfway between colors 1 and 2. A clean and useable wall color with sandy undertones.

5 An excellent "dirty" off-white. Good for "historic" interiors. Has an umber cast.

6 A warmer off-white than color 5, with a purplish cast. Good with deep warm color schemes.

7 Warm umber gray. An excellent "antiquing" color, being suggestive of dust.

8 A cool umber gray, suggestive of dark concrete. Excellent on walls and powerful.

9 The most delicate off-white here (printing limitations prevent the accurate reproduction

of really pale colors), warm and slightly old-looking.

10 Between the dirtiest of whites and umber gray. A very useable wall color, but perhaps less appealing if you decide to call it "Mushroom".

11 Cooler than color 7, an excellent gray made with white and raw umber—not black. Consequently very approachable, sophisticated, and useable. A color of concrete.

12 A deep tint of umber, redolent, like many swatches on this page, of suede, stone, or fur. This is a color with luxurious connotations.

period colors

ABOVE: Skansen is a museum village in Sweden in which houses and cottages of various periods and styles have been brought from all over the country, including this interior, which is an essay in the art of painting with green. Note how yellowish and bluish greens are combined.

VIEW THIS PALETTE WITH THE GRAY VIEWER

1 A deep green, almost black, that was famously employed in the eighteenth century for painting railings and fences, hence its name: "Railing Green". The color is lost against shaded foliage.

Many of these colors are bluish greens; in fact, it is interesting how fresh these colors seem and how few greens of the period had any noticeable yellowish glare.

2 A warm muddy green with plenty of period overtones. A cooler version of it has been found on woodwork at Trinity Church, Newport, Rhode Island, made from Prussian blue, verdigris, and white lead.

3 Described as "Mineral Green", a name often associated with the mineral pigment malachite. However, the color probably came from a processed copper chloride or Brunswick green.

4 A grayer tint of color 2 and a more delicately "antiqued" color. Complex and very useable.

5 Was in use throughout Europe. It's a useable, warm green made with yellow ochre.

6 A tint of a pigment known as "Green Verditer" (which was much more readily manufactured than its blue version—see over). A deep minty green.

7 Commonly known as "Pea Green", this is similar to a woodwork color at the William Trent House (1719) in Trenton, New Jersey.

8 A tint of color 6, this is a clean and pure color of great luminosity. Redolent of 1930s, 1830s, and 1730s interiors.

O h, the endless trauma of getting the right period color that doesn't make your house look like a museum. How do you do it? First by dispelling a myth. The popular view of historical colors (fuelled in most cases by visits to old buildings and looking at paintings of period interiors) is that in the past interior decoration was dull, dirty, and intolerably gloomy. This perception comes mainly from the way in which many paints deteriorate and discolor with age and partly because of the burgeoning number of "dirty", supposedly historical, paint ranges around.

The truth is somewhat different. Our forebears loved color, although only those who could afford it bought bright colors, a fact that underlines how expensive bright pigments were until the late nineteenth century and how class-related color schemes were.

This palette of forty colors, all authenticated and researched by the colorist and historian Patrick Baty, contains several popular "common" colors made from cheap pigments and a considerable number of mid-price colors, all from the eighteenth and early nineteenth centuries. Many of these colors were used across Europe and the United States; many are earlier; many are still popular today.

9, 10, 11 and 12 These are colors that sit between blue and gray and which are of obvious appeal for their ambiguity. Colors 9, 10 and 11 are tints of the same bluish gray that could be easily created by mixing a form of carbon black made from burnt vegetation into white paint. Burnt vine wood yielded the nicest blues. Color 12 is subtler and less steely in character. Their cool subtlety makes them very useable.

13 This is the color of cobalt glass frit, which served a unique purpose for strewing over wet oil paint to produce an intense sparkling blue, particularly on metalwork, known as "Smalt Blue". Modern ultramarine blue pigment will produce this color.

14, 15 and 16 These colors are clearer blues that were prized, being pigmented with blue verditer. The process of making this pigment, a by-product of silver refining, had been perfected in England in the seventeenth century and it was extensively used in oil and in distemper for walls as a "fair blew". It was later superseded by Prussian blue and synthetic ultramarine. Color 14 is similar to one found on woodwork in the Independence Hall, Philadelphia (1732–48). Color 15 was sometimes known as "Blue Verditer" and 16 as "Sky Blue". It's a lighter version of a color found at the Charles Carroll house, Annapolis, Maryland of the 1730s. All three colors are immensely useable, especially with the grayer swatches to the left.

Note that the swatches in this section are representative and cannot in every case convey the exact nuance of what are often highly complex colors. They should also not be read as definitive absolutes but as "rungs" on a ladder of tints. Hence, any color could be justifiably lighter or darker. These colors are available as paints: see the entry in "Notes on the Palettes" on page 177. Refer also to palettes 18 and 19 for early twentieth-century and 1920s colors.

VIEW THIS PALETTE WITH THE GRAY VIEWER

ABOVE: When used as part of a more complex palette, blues come alive. The late Denis Severs precisely manipulated color at his museum/house in Spitalfields, London, England, shown here. See the Northern Light palette 50 for examples of pinks and earth colors that combine with blues in this palette to produce similar combinations.

17, 18, 19, and 20 These colors are variously pigmented versions of ochre and sienna earth colors, producing beautiful, complex creams and stone colors. Many variations existed. Color 17 was known as "Roman Ochre", while a yellower version was referred to as "Spruce Oker"; when muddied, it was called "Oak" or "Wainscot color". Color 18 is a delicately balanced tint of a lemon color, cool and useable, especially in south-facing rooms. Color 19 was described as "Dutch Pink" (from the middle seventeenth-century word "pink", which was used to describe a particular yellow made from a vegetable dye lake. The word "lake" was used for red dye pigments, and "pink" was often used for yellow ones. Its previous definition had been "a very small thing", coming probably from the early Dutch word for "small": "pinck". In the eighteenth century "pink" also meant the height of perfection. Smith in the 1670s refers to the color as "Pink-yellow"). Color 20 is a classic cream made with yellow ochre and white: warm, pure, and useable in even a north-facing room.

21, 22, 23, and 24 These colors are warm grays and steely blues, reminiscent of bright and tarnished silver. It's worth obscuring the columns on either side to appreciate the delicacy of these tints, made with raw umber, white, and blue.

25, 26, 27, and 28 These swatches show a typical range of tints that could be produced from common hematite iron oxides such as red ochre. Like the earthy yellows, the stone colors, and the browns, these were cheap "common" colors.

29

33

37

30

34

38

31

35

39

32

36

40

29, 30, 31, and 32 These colors suggest names like "putty", "drab", or just "dirt". Color 31 was in fact sometimes called "Dark Stone" and color 32 "Olive color". It's similar to a color found on woodwork at Gunston Hall, Lorton, Virginia (built in the 1750s).

33, 34, 35, and 36 These colors, like all those on this page, were achieved with relatively simple pigments, most of them cheap powdered earths: Spanish brown and red, umbers, raw

and burnt sienna, and yellow ochre, mixed of course with white (chalk and lime for walls or lead carbonate for oil paint) and sometimes a little soot black. They made inexpensive and widely available paint. No wonder they were often called "common colors". Color 34 was enticingly named "Chocolate", while color 36 is similar to a color called "Walnut Tree".

37, 38, 39, and 40 These colors are more popular eighteenth- and early nineteenth-

century tints. Color 37 is another warm gray. Color 38 is a hilarious (and to our eyes overpowering) puce called "Peach Blossom color", color 39 is a more useable and grayed tint of it. Color 40 is a complex and beautiful indigo gray. Although there is hardly any evidence for this pigment being used in commercial house painting in the UK, it has been found in paints in America, France (as "Bleu de Lectour"), and elsewhere.

VIEW THIS PALETTE WITH THE GRAY VIEWER

OPPOSITE: More color sensibility from the late Denis Severs's house in Spitalfields, London, England. Cream and off-white are used to modulate an otherwise sugary pink.

ABOVE: The Homewood House Museum (1801–6) at the Johns Hopkins University, Baltimore, Maryland is decorated with an archetypal combination of period colors: soft mint and pea greens, and cool clean pale blues among others. These were not common colors, but polite and rarified tints for a discerning palate.

18 early twentieth-century colors

1 "Oxford Blue", a standard "clubbish" and now institutionalized color.

2 Brilliant green, unmistakeably nothing else.

3 Peacock blue, an unusually complex dark color and rather sophisticated placed against some of the other colors here.

4 Light "Battleship Gray", a useable gray because it contains brown to warm the color.

5 Dark blue, a deep cobalt color, used full strength.

6 Slate, a beautiful, complex, dark, and warm gray.

7 Turquoise blue, a complex and grayed version of turquoise, the color of the sea. All these blues work beautifully together as a palette of four equally intense hues.

8 Eau de nil, perhaps a typical green of the period.

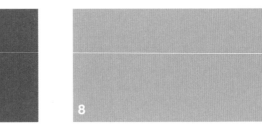

These are paint colors of the first few decades of the twentieth century, taken from a wider standard range of the time. To some extent they represent international taste, simply because the colors were developed not just by paint manufacturers, decorators, and architects, but also by engineers, the military, and shipbuilders, all of whom were interested in codifying color. As a result of advances in pigment technology in the nineteenth century, it had only recently become possible to use a wide range of colors that were cheap and permanent. The resulting agreed collection of colors, which was British, was the first standardized paint range to be published.

It predictably contained colors such as "Signal Red" and light and dark "Battleship Gray", which were developed in World War I. But surprisingly there were many more approachable tints and shades with more romantic names that were suitable for domestic decoration: "Light Indian Red", "French Gray", "Azure", "Salmon Pink", "Quaker Gray", and "Sea Green".

Because these sixteen colors are taken from a range, not a "palette", of colors, there is no obvious cohering structure to relate them all to each other, save two things: a preponderance of brown colors and a chromatic intensity that even the pale colors share. Compare this palette with palette 19, a collection of decorating colors from the late 1920s.

9 "Signal Red", a new and important hue then, has won its spurs as an invaluable signage and branding color around the globe.

10 Salmon, a virulent tint that needs strong other colors around it.

11 Venetian red, a good orange-biased iron oxide color, typically arranged with the other colors in this column or with colors 4 and 6.

12 Middle brown. A good warm brown, useful for "anchoring" other colors.

13 Deep buff. Use this color as the key component of a four-color palette with the swatches below and to the right.

14 Pale cream. Interestingly, this early twentieth-century cream is dirty, while those of the eighteenth century (see palette 17) are entirely clean and fresh.

15 Deep cream. Cleaner than color 14, but still with a muddy hint.

16 Primrose. A cool yellow, actually beloved in all periods. An interesting palette can be made using this and the other three colors in the bottom row.

ABOVE: This miner's kitchen from a house in the English Midlands has remained unaltered since the early twentieth century. Colors 4 and 15 from the preceding pages would help in recreating it.

ABOVE: The kitchen in William and Walter Shaw's house, Nottinghamshire. The bay-fronted three-story Edwardian villa is like thousands of others built at the turn of the twentieth century. William and Walter lived here for fifty years. They preserved the house as it was when their parents died in the 1930s. They ignored modern conveniences such as central heating, the telephone, and television. The house features 1920s wallpapers, Victorian furniture, and household objects. Standard lowly paints such as colors 2 and 8 (brilliant green and eau de nil shown here) would have been widely available for this expanding housing market.

1 A pretty bluish green similar to some of the eighteenth-century colors. Clean and uncomplicated. Its blue-green ambiguity means it is a cusp color.

2 This delicate pink is of the sort made with an Indian/Spanish-type native red ochre, which gives it a bluish cast. Also a cusp color.

3 A very slightly gray yellow, a chalky tint of primrose yellow. Could appear green in some lights.

4 A delicate clean watery violet color. Good with the cool pink, blue color 5, or pale blue color 7.

5 A very useable and pale indigo gray-blue, and an important one. Use it as a predominant color in combination with detail/secondary use of any other colors in this palette.

6 An uncomplicated baby blue. Guileless.

7 Almost gray, the kind of pale blue that can be made with vegetable black pigment and white.

8 Light olive green, good with the pinks above and right.

9 This orange ochre-pink is a typical Art Deco color,

particularly in conjunction with the more sludgy colors in this palette.

10 A cool and very slightly purplish gray. Unusual and good in combination with its equally muted complementary, color 8, or the pinks here.

11 Another unusual color, a slightly dusty bronze brown.

12 Glaucous sea green. Ambiguous and a cusp color.

VIEW THIS PALETTE WITH THE GRAY VIEWER

ABOVE: This palette is a collection of shell colors, mother-of-pearl and the iridescent sheen of silver leaf. These delicate ideas and materials were essential components of early Art Deco schemes and the 1920s rococo typified in this room.

This is a palette of paint colors from the mid-1920s and one that, although sampled from paint colors from the period (taken from manufacturers' color cards), possesses a fascinating coherence, a character that unwittingly and succinctly epitomizes the time. In fact all the "palettes" (or collections of colors) in this period chapter do the same: the eighteenth-century palette is deep and clear, biased to blue, gray, and orange; the early 1900s palette is rich and slightly muddied with an emphasis on brown and dark principal hues. This palette has a very complex character: it is slightly muddied, hazy, and grayed, and tonally extremely light. These colors are very appealing to modern taste because they are not too strong and difficult to use. They are pastel tints, redolent of the Art Deco period that they precede and innocent of the brooding quality of colors that predated World War I.

Although the paler tints are sugary, they're all slightly toned by the addition of a little gray and are presented against deeper and more complex colors such as olive green, dusty chocolate, and glaucous blue-green-grays. On the next page are one or two darker colors of the period. These also have muted characters.

13 A magnolia orange-tinged pink. This is an almost impossible color to use by itself but it's very useful with the strong clear greens below.

14 A deeper tint of the same color. This palette is really all about a much older game: the complementary relationship of red and green, explored elsewhere in this book (see palettes 41, 43 and 55).

15 Pale gray-green, a delicate and clean pale minty color. Use combined with the color below.

16 Gray-green. This is the kind of chrysocolla "Mountain Green" that Nero is said to have strewn across the floor of the Coliseum before appearing on it dressed in the same color as a proclamation of self-renewal. It may well have a calming and balancing psychological effect; it certainly suggests vitality and growth.

ABOVE: This sitting room, in Virginia Woolf's home at Monk's House in East Sussex, is painted in her favorite color—one available from several contemporary paint ranges. It was vibrant and clean colors such as these that were adopted by artists in the Bloomsbury Group.

There is a more muscular side to 1920s design and decoration, rooted, not in period revival, but in the vibrant late nineteenth-century traditions of the Arts and Crafts movement, and swayed by continental, American, and even primitive African influences. The Art Deco movement found its energy and abstraction in primitive art and applied pattern—from Assyrian sculpture to tribal painting and Egyptian architecture. The intellectual and artistic movements of the time were equally spellbound by primitivism, only they were less entranced by the trappings and baubles of these cultural sources than by their magic and superstition. This palette, like the others for this period, is taken from a commercial color card of the time. But these are not the cheap utilitarian workers' colors of World War I, colors that seemed simply an incidental side effect of the protective paint layer. Nor are they just a trivial and gay Art Deco palette for cinema decoration. They point to something new, which is more fully explored on the next page. They speak of a refreshed, clean world, postwar, and an interest in the ancient magical properties of color to heal and restore the soul.

VIEW THIS PALETTE WITH THE GRAY VIEWER

ABOVE: This Los Angeles home employs color in a complex and confident way. Note that all the colors used are in some way "off": dirtied by brown or black. This trick homogenizes them all.

17 A rich, grayed cream that still manages to retain some warmth. That's quite some feat.

18 A pretty pale warm gray. Use with the green or the blues.

19 This typical 1920s green was called "Mignonette" by the manufacturer. Bluish, complex, and useable.

20 Fancifully called "Persian Red", an intense and slightly shaded cool red. Try it with just the color above and below for a very "informed" look.

21 A complex blue but one that is still intense. Called "Myosotis Blue". These exotic names suggest a rather sophisticated approach to color.

22 "Sky blue", apparently a simple clear tint, but in fact a complex balance of white, blue, gray, and green. Very useable.

If Art Deco colors were guileless and Bohemian 1920s taste ran to vibrant hues and tints, then serious architects were pursuing yet another color story. Although we think of Modernism, that great 1920s invention, as a monochrome visual language, that is nearly always because photographs of Modernist buildings were in black-and-white. In fact many interwar new buildings were colored—on the outside as well as in.

These six swatches are less innocent than those on the preceding page: they are all shaded with a little black. It's as though this palette has been muted for a more sober use. The colors certainly suggest the influence of building materials such as wood, stone, and cement. Or if you like, references from other cultures: Oriental ceramics, tribal wood carvings, and Roman wall paintings. That's where these colors also appear.

Whichever way you look at it, this is a grown-up palette with serious intentions. It looks very sophisticated when used in an interior such as the one shown opposite.

VIEW THIS PALETTE WITH THE GRAY VIEWER

I f you remove the greens from this page (especially the lime green) you're left with an uncontroversial but rather beautifully composed set of colors. Add the greens and you have an Art Deco Miami palette or a typical late-1990s popular paint range as sold in DIY superstores: colors that are slightly shaded with a little black or toned with a little gray.

But this palette doesn't come from Miami or from the 1990s. It is derived from sophisticated interior design schemes from New York in the 1940s, a decade when brown, to an extent, dominated design of all kinds. The six colors below formed a proposed scheme for a dining room (opposite there is one more proposal) where the brown-gray was to be the predominant wall color. That recommendation is probably one worth following.

Opposite are four colors proposed for a library: a somber scheme tinged with blue, brown, and purple and heightened with scarlet for line or detail. This is a sharp set of colors with no hint of the musty associations of the 1940s (or libraries for that matter). It's one funky palette.

1 A neutral pale "donkey" color similar to John Fowler's pet wall color of the period, "Mouse's Back". Very useable, particularly without all the colors below or in combination with the blue and violets.

2 A tiny quantity of black takes the lurid edge off this green. Look at this with just the blue below and brown left.

3 A good complex blue that can be used with off-white and the colors above and below.

4 You can build a very dynamic combination with this clean turquoise green, the violet below, and the lime green, in contrast to the other three, much softer tints.

5 All the colors in this column have a similar tonal value that connects what are otherwise disparate hues. The brown-gray and this tint bracket the cleaner color in between.

6 Build a palette with only these lower four colors, or mask this violet for a three-color palette of even greater innocence.

VIEW THIS PALETTE AGAINST WHITE OR WITH THE GRAY VIEWER

LEFT: It's not surprising to find very modern design that echoes—or just copies—color ways and schemes from historical periods. By delving into the past and raiding it, a designer can imbue a product, a building, or an interior with a magical extra value: the subtle echo of an association with something other than the here and now. Like all the pictures in this book, this one was found after the palette had been researched and compiled.

7 A typical early twentieth-century dark "Battleship Gray" and a good lead or slate color.

8 Cooler than the pale violet on the opposite page and a pivotal color between the swatches above and below.

9 A complex and interesting mixture of violet, gray, and brown that will change character according to prevailing lighting conditions (a cusp color). This and color 8 are wonderful and important colors that give this palette of four real maturity.

10 An uncompromising scarlet or vermilion red that is moving toward orange. Try the other three colors without this one for a safer combination.

This is the 1950s embodied! Here and in the next spread are three archetypal British palettes of the time, based on interior schemes by Raymond Rust and Lucienne Day. In palette 22, the scheme ideas are more muted and subtly resolved; the colors on this page are louder and, for the period, intense.

All speak eloquently for that decade, not least because, of the five colors assembled here and the eight overleaf, ten have some degree of black in them—even the pink, which is slightly shaded. The exceptions are the two yellows opposite and the one overleaf, which, if tinged with black, would markedly change in perceived color toward a sludgy green.

1 This is a pale and innocent primrose yellow that is likely to turn immediately to green if it even gets a whiff of gray or black. Use on top of the red or green for best effect.

2 The main core tension of this palette is the red/green complementary effect, although it has been restrained by muting the hues of these colors with gray.

3 This is a complex and useable green, an equable mixture of green, yellow, and black that is particularly good when just used with the primrose yellow, above.

4 The secondary core tension of this palette is the contrast effect of black versus yellow. A difficult color to use by itself, but an important part of this scheme.

5 Not only is black used to shade colors in these palettes, it also appears as a solid color. Here it also sets off the yellow.

ABOVE: Perhaps no twentieth-century architect has experimented so widely with color as Le Corbusier. This is his Villa Sarabhai in India. There's a genetic link—a similarity in the use of black to slightly stain a color—between this scheme and colors from the 1920s (palette 19).

VIEW THIS PALETTE AGAINST WHITE

1 This is a very slight gray with just enough yellow in it to relate to the colors below. Probably a good color for indoor decoration.

2 Another, rare, color with no black in it. Like the yellow on the previous page, this green has an aggressive relationship with the black, although this whole palette is less dynamic.

3 An important color in this palette because it bridges the green-yellow and the black.

4 Black is again used as a solid element in this scheme, as well as a shading element in other colors.

5 This gray casts a slight shadow over the whole palette. Obliterate it to gauge its effect.

6 There is a small quantity of black in this pink— which takes the sugary edge off it. Carefully used, this is an unusual and effective decorating color.

7 A very useable color, soft and gray enough to be versatile. Particularly good with just the pink as a slightly tarnished "baby" scheme. Mmmm.

8 A bronze green, the color of dead moss and clearly the pivotal color in this scheme, with or without black.

Just as many decorating colors of the 1940s were cast with a brown content (see palette 20), so brighter colors were being introduced in the 1950s after a period of relative austerity. So it's not surprising to find designers modulating them a little in order to make them accessible. It's interesting to compare the colors on these pages with the equivalently muted tones of printed color media of the 1950s, such as magazines (see palette 42), where technological limitations resulted in both poor color reproduction and an excess of black and gray on the page. It's also interesting to see how the British textile designer Lucienne Day in the 1950s was using pink and bronze together—in a way that fellow British textile designer, Eddie Squires, was to do more vibrantly in the 1960s (see palette 24).

VIEW THIS PALETTE WITH THE GRAY VIEWER

This retro house in London designed by Jenny Armit contains some pivotal early 1950s colors that by then had enjoyed a developing role in design for some thirty years: cool yellow, bronze green, very soft pale cool cream, and pink, gray, gray-blue, and of course black.

1 A clean, cool, and intense pink. Its naïveté is typical of the 1960s.

2 A stronger Pink Panther tint of the same color.

3 Slightly greenish, this bronze color is pivotal to the entire palette. Use it also with just the pinks to give them a veneer of depth and interest, or with just the brick red and purple for a more severe and savory palette.

4 This brick red is slightly evasive: dusty, brown-tinged and veering toward orange. Its ambiguity means that it performs differently according to prevailing lighting conditions (a cusp color).

5 This purplish plum exerts a powerful controlling effect over the pinks, even when used in small quantities. It also has a difficult, strident relationship with the brick red (they can be used together to disconcerting effect and their relationship moderated with the bronze).

In came the 1960s and out went black, to be replaced by, well, not brown but bronze. Brown, it must be said, can often work as an anchoring color in a palette, not just because it's a dark and indeterminate color, but because it is the color nearly always obtained by mixing two complementary hues. A "useful" brown will veer either toward a principal color in a palette or toward its complementary. So, in a palette of blues, a brown made with yellow or orange (complementaries of blue) will have a more heightening effect than one made with green or red (which are close to blue).

This palette uses brown—or bronze—with a delicate poise. The color is yellowish brown with a hint of green that if it were any more intense would strike the eye as an obvious complementary of magenta—the hue from which the two pinks are derived. The central position of the pinks is reinforced by two near colors, the brick red and purple: together they form a phalanx of cool and warm red-based colors all ranked in the subtlest of opposition to the bronze color.

In short this is a palette of delicate tints with relationships that are half-hidden. Not surprisingly, these colors are from one of the masters of '60s commercial coloring, Eddie Squires, who used them together in wallpaper designs. There are more on the next spread.

VIEW THIS PALETTE AGAINST WHITE OR WITH THE GRAY VIEWER

OPPOSITE: Bronze mustn't be underestimated as an anchoring or a complementary color. Here it's pulling the same stunt with red and pink for Tricia Guild as it did for Eddie Squires in the 1960s.

1 This deep ultrablue is a sharp foil for (and near complementary of) the orange and of the magenta pink in this palette, but it's also the outsider here. Experiment with varying amounts of this color.

2 A deep hue, no-holds-barred full-force orange that partners the magenta in the lead role in this palette. Both can be used together with just the blue or just the bronze colors.

3 This bronze brown in fact contains a high proportion of orange. Consequently it's quite amiable to the colors on either side of it but is an effective complementary brown for the blue.

4 Another intense full-hue color, a slightly warm magenta, partner to the orange.

5 This color could be called moss green or bronze green. Either way, its yellowish tinge places it in the direct complementary path of the magenta, although its brownish complexity weakens the effect. These two colors can be used to great effect by themselves.

ABOVE The Paris home of Florence Baudoux, a furniture and accessories designer, is a twenty-first-century retro dream. The "Long Stripe" sofa is from Florence's own Oom collection. The leather "PK22" chairs are by Poul Kjaerholm. The chairs around the table are Eames side shells. Note the extensive use of bronze on the walls to calm this riotous scheme down.

Here are five more colors from Eddie Squires. The bronze and pink combination reworks the ideas explored on the previous page but this time with stronger hues (and so stronger complementary browns). The blue and orange combination is added here because it shows just how far the man was prepared to go when it came to putting complementary colors together: these two hues—Prussian blue and a wholly synthetic orange—are just about as intense and pure as color can get.

Seen as a palette of five colors, the orange and magenta scream get up and go. Thank goodness for those bronze swatches. They know how to keep everything under control.

VIEW THIS PALETTE AGAINST WHITE OR WITH THE GRAY VIEWER

An apartment in a 1950s block in New York's Gramercy Park. The floor is poured epoxy resin in sky blue. The orange chair was designed by David Khouri. It all has an other-worldly, super-retro feel, and is indebted to the progressive use of intense pigments in the 1960s.

1 A bright chrome yellow (but made with a new generation of synthetic dye pigments). Clean, intense, and uncompromising. The orange tinge to this color means it won't tend to green in poor lighting conditions. Very similar to yellows used internationally in signage and on construction/ infrastructure equipment.

2 A slightly muddier version of the color to the left, this yellow approaches the color ochre. Its muted hue means it will form a well-anchored relationship with any other color on this page, especially colors 4, 5, and 6.

3 A beautiful, warm, and brilliant orange, again uncompromising, but less industrial in its associations than the yellow, above. Try it alone with the green, blue, or especially the cherry red, below right.

4 An almost pure red. Difficult to handle by itself, but try it with the orange, left, or the green, its subtractive complementary.

5 A slightly burnt orange that as a result is easier to use and less strident than the color above. It takes on a new vitality when placed against the green or the blue.

6 A light cherry red, a toned red that is moving slightly toward purple and so has a cooler cast than the red above. Try them together and watch the internecine struggle of two advancing colors thrashing it out.

7 A deep emerald green, difficult to use by itself but especially good with the oranges and orange-red above.

8 A clear intense blue that is tending slightly to green. Especially good against color 3, its complementary, or the darker orange color 5. Or try these colors plus the yellows.

These eight colors belong to plastic fantastic. They are the groovy, intense—and permanent—hues of the psychedelic generation. I mention permanent because these colors did not just appear as the hallucinatory result of some designer hippy trip. They were in fact the outcome of several decades of research. Bright synthetic pigments had been around since the beginning of the twentieth century, and bright synthetic dyes from the 1860s, but many of them were fugitive: they faded. For the color chemist, the holy grail of color synthesis remained a range of artificial pigments resistant to chemical and ultraviolet effect; and by the 1960s, developments in petrochemicals, plastics, and dye manufacturing had made such a range possible. It's interesting that we associate such colors with the hippy generation of the late 1960s, whereas these colors were available much earlier. Some occur in late 1950s interiors; most of them date from early 1960s furniture; and one, color 5, dates from 1946.

The cleaner colors are the top four and, if you like, can be used as a palette together. The four below are slightly shaded and also work well as a group. Note the juxtaposition of the similar yellows, red, and oranges. When used together, these close vibrant colors make the eyes do a lot of work, appearing to move and shimmer.

VIEW THIS PALETTE AGAINST WHITE

natural palettes

ABOVE: This was a popular palette in the later neoclassical eighteenth century. (Wedgwood was after all only supplying ceramic goods in the popular architectural colors of the time.) The fashion set for these delicate tints in England and France was then adopted throughout Europe, particularly in Scandinavia. This is Bernshammar in Sweden.

1 A pale and delicate Wedgwood blue that historically has found much use as a decorative color, being nearly gray. Exquisite. It should be used much more.

2 This misty reddish purple is the anchoring color for this palette. Surprisingly, purple often is.

3 and 4 Both these deeper tints are also very effective decorative colors, although they are best employed as part of this overall palette.

This a very balanced set of colors. The original source is Wedgwood colored ware, but this palette is lifted from the 1937 edition of Parsons's *Historical Colours*, a volume that says as much about the taste of the interwar years as it does about any of its historical references. These four colors are presented here, on one page together, all equally milky and grayed. It is as though they were being seen through a soft-focus gauze filter.

Similar milky colors can be found in palette 59. This palette works by taking three tints of a neutral mid-blue that are underpinned by a purple, deeper in tone and relatively distant from the blue, since the purple is moving toward red. It's a clear case of purple being used as an anchor in the palette, a device that pops up surprisingly often in the history of design and hence in this book.

27 a Norse legend

1 A slightly greenish warm gray, useful against all the colors below and a very useful decorating color, both as a wall color and as a deep off-white for woodwork and ceilings.

2 A clear and slightly purplish blue, very sharp and cool. Useful against the blues and greens below.

3 This subtle gray-blue has great character in a decorative scheme. It has an almost lavender tinge.

4 This is a very solid, dense green that nevertheless works to great effect when used in small quantities against the other colors. Or try it as the dominant color.

5 Do not underestimate the power of purple in a palette. This may be a subtle version, but despite its quietness, it has a pivotal role here. Cover it to see for yourself. Especially striking against its complementary: the green, above right.

6 An intense smoky turquoise green that is chromatically far removed from the color above. Another pivotal color in this palette: try it with just the colors in this column or as part of the four lower colors. A very exciting color.

7 In contrast to color 3, this is a cooler blue—but still toned with gray. Use it as an antidote to the greens and also as part of a four-color palette in this column only.

8 A subtler and less blue version of the color above, this is a cusp color that changes character according to different lighting conditions. Especially good when subdued with large quantities of color 3.

This is the palette of a summer landscape and sky: a landscape where the greens are hazy and shift toward blue in the middle distance, and where the blues are soft and light, the colors of cloud and mildly overcast skies. They are, in short, the outdoor colors belonging to a temperate climate and similar in feeling to the "Northern Light" palette 50.

These colors bring opportunities for all kinds of combinations of varying character. Nearly every one is subtly muted with an adjacent hue plus brown or gray. So, the greens are a little muddied and are mixed with either yellow or blue, and the blues are a little muddied and are mixed with either purple or green. As a result, almost any combination of these colors will be interesting. The exception to this principle is of course the gray, which is brown-green tinged.

That this palette comes from Scandinavian interiors shouldn't surprise anyone. These colors—and rooms containing them—were well-publicized and featured in magazines throughout the 1980s and 1990s. What is interesting is how many Scandinavian interiors, especially those of the eighteenth and nineteenth centuries, make use of these landscape colors with a lightness of touch and sensitivity for their aerial quality.

ABOVE: Lena Proudlock, a Swede living abroad, designed this kitchen in what can only be described as her native style. It makes use of a great deal of white combined with some of the colors in this palette.

VIEW THIS PALETTE AGAINST WHITE

ABOVE: The walls of artist potter Rupert Spira's house in Shropshire, England, were stenciled in about 1830. Other rooms in this home appear elsewhere in this book (see palettes 50 and 53). All illustrate the same grayed subtlety in the colors that can be found in this palette.

There are several palettes in this book that are marine. Some come from the turquoise Aegean, others from the coast of Africa. Others harbor the limpid colors of a Scandinavian or American seascape. There are several other palettes in this book that reflect the colors of the sky: aerial gray-blues, deep cobalt summer hues, or the muted tones of northern skies.

This palette is a subtler collection of softened, blended tints and tones, the ambiguous colors of a midocean seascape. It does both marine and aerial. That's because it comes straight from the navy and air force; or rather, this is a selection of colors that sailors and airmen have had their boats and planes painted since World War II in countries around the world. Separately, they are functional colors. Put together, they are beautiful.

1 A generic camouflage green that is satisfyingly grayed and complex. A color suggestive of deep-dyed green wool, or suede, because it has a slightly dusty quality. Use with the colors immediately around it for a combination that is mature and sophisticated.

2 The deep color of duck eggs and a hazy gray-green-blue tint that is part aerial, part aqueous. A delightful 1940s and 1950s decorating color, good for walls, to be mixed with the color to its right.

3 Another period twentieth-century color, although harder and deeper than color 2. Use as an accent color with it, or with the other colors in this column.

4 This is a delightful warm gray but with no nasty brown "mushroom" connotations. A very useable color, especially with color 2, or with off-white.

5 A good deep smoky gray with the requisite touch of blue. A good contemporary furniture color and good with the other colors in this column.

6 Another aerial and atmospheric light blue to use with the other colors in this column, or for a less naive and classier combination, with the colors in this row. Much more interesting because it's a cusp color that changes identity according to the prevailing light.

7 A flexible color that willl work with any other on this page. Beautiful. The color of deep seawater.

8 A real seascape color, part green, part blue, and mainly gray. A fabulous, complex color to use with any other on this page. An important anchoring color for this palette.

9 A guileless cool blue tone, slightly grayed and very fine with colors 2 and 4.

10 The kind of hard bluish gray produced by mixing carbon black and white pigment. Good with the other colors in this column.

11 Another one of those deep ambiguous colors that seems to have everything else thrown in it: smoky, oily with a hint of luminous green. This color will appear black when used in small quantities, deep and powerful when used over large areas.

12 There is the vaguest hint of warmth to this blue that makes it difficult to use with many of the green-tinged colors on these pages. Best paired with colors 4 and 8.

VIEW THIS PALETTE WITH THE GRAY VIEWER

In an Oliver Hill 1930s house in Frinton-on-Sea, England, this suitably retro interior (designed by its owner, the furniture collector Andrew Weaving) is held together by a warm organic palette. It brings what is otherwise a white box alive.

1 Deep forest green, the shadow color of foliage. Velvety and rich.

2 Deep moss green, matt and brown-tinged. Use it with the deep forest green, left.

3 This is a very useable color, a warm stone gray similar to the concrete colors in palette 30). A cooler version of color 5, opposite, with which it can be used in a sophisticated combination.

4 A chestnut brown to lift the two greens above. A good soil color or that of deep tanned pigskin and suede. Very good with the violet color 12, opposite.

5 A warmer color than color 3 but still a good stone. Use in abundance with all the colors in this palette.

6 An unusual sandy-green-yellow, a sort of khaki drab that has a suede quality. Use with colors 5, 7 and 8 at the top of this page to lighten it.

7 This deep ochre underwrites these top four colors and also works with the four colors below it.

8 Warmer than the color above it, but this color needs the yellow, left, and red, below, to kick-start it into any kind of life. If this drab swatch can be described as anything, it is organic.

9 If you take all the colors in this palette together, the colors that take a positive, proactive role are colors 3, 6, 8, and this one, a warm terra-cotta. The color of sand dunes at sunset, hence chosen by the SAS in the 1991 Gulf War for their Land Rovers.

10 Brick brown, that with the violet below, wakes up the colors above and makes a really interesting arrangement out of this column.

11 Darker than color 1, great with the colors around it and when viewed only with the other swatches in this column.

12 The most interesting color in this palette, deep and with the same dusty quality that many of these colors share. Where purple appears in a palette, it often takes a pivotal role. Brown sometimes takes the same role. Here it is shared between them. Try pairing colors 4, 10, or 12 with any other single color here to see some interesting combinations.

From mossy rocks to deep forest, wooded hillsides to open moorland, these are the colors of the great outdoors, a wilderness palette of rustic colors: foliage, earth, sand, and rock. They are deeper and lusher than the colors of the savannah (see palette 32) or those of the earth (see palette 31). Mineral colors are here, but they're balanced by the greens of deep summer—or jungle—foliage.

These are colors for posh country front doors or the colors that farmers should paint their grain silos and slurry tanks, and for good reason. Every swatch on this page is taken from a selection of military camouflage schemes covering the last sixty years.

VIEW THIS PALETTE WITH THE GRAY VIEWER

ABOVE: You might have thought this palette so off-the-wall that we couldn't find an interior to illustrate it. But here's a rather funky 1950s dining room that encapsulates the colors here. Even the yellow is there.

1 One of the available colors of red oxide paint, this color is a warm, orange-tinged red suitable for outdoor work.

2 Pale mid-neutral gray, the color of galvanized (zinc-dipped) steel and of micaceous iron oxide gray primer used on steelwork everywhere. Also a concrete color.

3 This warm gray is almost beige. A good concrete color when used with the other grays on this page and a very approachable decorating color.

4 A darker version of the color to the left and another good color for the home.

5 A mid-warm concrete color, pinker than the other two.

6 Bright and warm chrome/cadmium yellow, the color of construction machinery. Try covering this swatch to radically alter the palette.

7 A warm iron oxide color with plenty of orange in it. Another good exterior (and historic furniture color). A pale color of rust.

8 Deeper rust and also the color of the Red Iron of Oxide paint used for 120 years to paint the Forth Bridge in Scotland (incidentally).

It might be difficult to guess where this palette comes from. Perhaps the yellow betrays the source. These are all everyday colors from civil engineering, from construction sites, and from heavy manufacturing industry around the world. It is a familiar palette, taken from the colors of concrete, metal primers, rust, and of course the yellow of the construction plant. With or without the yellow, this is a very useable palette because of the warm neutralizing effect of the grays, the colors of warm-colored concrete. The color of concrete will vary according to the color of its components: rock, or aggregate, and sand. The base color of cement is a cold bluish gray, but as a material it is never employed alone. Color 2 is the coldest concrete color here.

VIEW THIS PALETTE WITH THE GRAY VIEWER

1 Correctly known just as ochre. Widely used, it is a strong muddy yellow that is usually more brilliant when mixed with a little white.

2 A tint of color 1. This is an immensely useable color in decoration and will appear a warm yellow when it reflects on itself in a room. Ochre is the only yellow with which to make a decent cream.

3 This color is that of a very warm and pure ochre of the highest quality, such as the best grades produced by the Roussillon mines in France. However, commercial "Golden Ochre" is often a mix of ordinary ochre and chrome yellow.

4 A tint of color 3. This looks correspondingly warmer, although when ochres and oxides are mixed with white pigments, their hue changes, turning slightly cooler. A deep creamy yellow, very useable.

5 A dark and cool red oxide with a purplish undertone. It has powerful tinting properties.

6 A tint of color 5. The purple undertone is clearer in a tint. Cool bluish pinks such as this have been used for centuries, especially indoors, partly because the color appears much cleaner and fresher than imaginable for an earth color and partly because the resulting tints are not "sugary".

7 Some hematites and ochreous earths produce much warmer, orange-tinged pigments that have always been more highly prized than the more common purplish varieties. Because it has no hard bluish edge, this color has often been used at full strength, for example to paint the city walls of Taroudant in Morocco and parts of Rome.

8 A tint of color 7. Tints of warm red ochres have a correspondingly warm bias. They occur on the exterior of buildings as part of a vernacular vocabulary throughout the world: in Morocco, India, Europe and Central America, and frequently appear in this book.

This is an oddball palette. It's not based on an object or place, nor an historic scheme. Nor is it representative of a color code or an artist's period palette. These colors belong to something called the "earth" palette, a collection of simple, cheap, totally permanent, and uncomplicated pigments that have been in use for tens of thousands of years and that are still widely available. Although not bright, they still form the basis of artists' palettes because of their delicate ambiguity and muddy tonality. These are properties of every earth color, creating a strong family likeness. As a result, this palette has an overall very coherent character.

The pigments rely (mainly) on simple iron compounds for their color—in other words rust. Because iron makes up the bulk mass of the planet, earth pigments can be easily mined all over the world, being often refined from clay or found in soft stone deposits. So not only are they historical colors, they are also international ones (although strong regional variations and combinations exist). Most interestingly, because these iron compounds also color our rock, sand, marbles, and soils, the colors of earth pigments take on those associations: buildings painted in them appear to immediately "root" themselves in the landscape. Earth pigments (like all mineral pigments) are mined in almost every country, so wide local variations of color occur. The swatches here are representative of the significant main types that have been recognized since Greek times and that are now codified as standard artists' colors. Read this palette in conjunction with "Early Period Colors" palette 17 for historical "common" colors that included earth pigments.

ABOVE: Earth pigments have an obvious role to play in "rooting" decorative schemes. Because of the big brown bias to the palette, an earth-based scheme will include other natural materials other than clay pigment, such as wood, terra-cotta, and stone. The last two, like many marbles, sands, and plasters, take their color from the very same oxides that color the pigments.

VIEW THIS PALETTE WITH THE GRAY VIEWER

9

13

17

21

ABOVE: The use of earth colors is universal and timeless. The pigments are so cheap and useful that now, as hundreds and thousands of years ago, they still form the basis of many paint ranges and are an important part of the artists' palette. Architecturally they pop up in all sorts of periods. This is a studiedly retro 1950s interior in London belonging to architectural historian Neil Bingham.

VIEW THIS PALETTE WITH THE GRAY VIEWER

9 Burnt sienna has become a standardized artists' pigment. It is a useful glazing color for transparent work and an invaluable pigment for marbling, wood graining, staining, and varnish work. It has a warmer, more brownish cast than some of the hematite red oxides.

10 A tint of color 9. When burnt sienna is mixed with white, it loses its fiery undertone and becomes cooler. Tints of this color are useful for suggesting the color of plaster or for mixing with yellow ochre for the color of terra-cotta. This is a restrained and cool earthy color with a hint of warmth about it.

11 Terra verde or green earth. This is a much less effectual color than the others, being pale, a weak colorant, and almost transparent in most media. Despite this, artists and decorators have persisted in using it because of its permanence and

cheapness, its qualities as a glazing pigment and its soft color (which varies enormously from bluish to yellowish according to the source). Most famously used in Greek icon and medieval tempera panel painting as the undercolor beneath flesh tones.

12 A tint of color 11. Because of this pigment's weak tinctorial power, it is almost useless when mixed with white.

13 Raw sienna. The pigment is rich, deep, and golden when used undiluted and is more opaque than ochre. As its name suggests, it is an "uncooked" or raw version of burnt sienna, deriving originally from the area around Siena in Umbria.

14 A tint of color 13. The best grades of this pigment produce a tint the color of manila envelopes, a rich warm beige. A very useable decorating color.

15 The name "Mars" indicates a synthetic iron oxide. Traditionally, naturally occurring purplish iron oxides have been processed and used in small quantities, although the color was often weak as represented here. Modern Mars violet is deeper than this.

16 A tint of color 15. A delicate grayish violet and very useable in decoration because the earthiness of this pigment prevents the color from looking too synthetic.

17 When raw sienna and raw umber are mixed, a neutral brown results that is similar to many shades of mined sienna and mined umber pigments. This is a useful color in decoration, a neutral muddy nothing brown for antiquing and aging other colors both when mixed with them and in a glaze or varnish coat.

18 A tint of color 17. This is a most versatile and useful earth tint for artists because it has a grayish

"dust"-like color without the coldness of a raw umber tint or the obvious "colored" warmth of a raw sienna tint. A beautiful wall color and one that appears in many regional/vernacular palettes in this book.

19 Orange ochre/Pozzuoli red/Mars orange. This is a dark color that was historically superseded by red lead (a bright orange), realgar, or orange-biased vermilion. However, there are many recorded cases of these more expensive pigments being adulterated with red earth pigments, for which an orange version would no doubt have been useful.

20 A tint of color 19. A good terra-cotta color.

21 Raw umber. This color is added to many pseudo-historical colors because it's very good at suggesting dirt. It does form the base of one or two deep sludge hues of the eighteenth century (see

also palette 17) and is a very useful toning/shading color when used in small quantities in mixes because of its cool neutrality.

22 A tint of color 21. Artists often prefer grays made with white and raw umber: the greenish brown bias is obscured and the resulting gray is warm and very useable.

23 Burnt umber. Raw and burnt umber take their name from Umbria in central Italy from where the finest grades once came. They complete the set of six basic modern earth colors. Burnt umber is deep, heavy, and chocolaty in character.

24 A tint of color 23. A gray pink-brown, a significant color of design and decoration in the 1940s (see also palette 20), although it occurs in many other periods.

1 A good color to suggest moderately bright bronze, a muted and ambiguous yellow-brown-green.

2 A very useable warm buff color with no nasty traces of orange. Like a piece of manila paper.

3 This is the cleanest color in this palette, an ochre cream that is essential to keep the whole palette from appearing too dingy.

4 A strong sage green, the color of ancient textiles overdyed with weld (yellow) on top of woad (blue). For other colors of this derivation see palette 44.

5 This moss/khaki color has enough blue and gray in it to make it useable and ambiguous. A possible cusp color.

6 A deeper version of color 5. Use with the other colors in this column, especially the brown, to control it.

7 A slightly greenish gasoline blue—or is it green? An interesting cusp color suggestive of a faded version of color 4, where the woad (blue) prevails.

8 A key color in this palette but also for the four lower colors by themselves. This is a rare thing: a very useable true brown; slightly greenish, slightly grayish.

These are savannah colors. The dried-out straw colors of grasses and sandy soil, the greens and browns of foliage, bark, and caked mud. These aren't clean colors (they are in fact all taken from Verdure tapestries). They have been made complex by the addition of brown or gray or a little of a color's complementary (which has the same effect), or by the pollution of a color's hue by the adjacent hue (such as color 7, which is a green that is almost blue). In fact, in every case a combination of complicated changes has affected the original hue, so that color 4, for example, is an emerald green, tinted with white, discolored with a little blue, and muted with brown and gray.

It is complex mutations such as this that make colors interesting (up to a point), especially when groups of such colors are brought together. By contrast, if this palette consisted of clean, simple browns, greens, and yellows, it would have seemed coarse and childlike. Instead, its complexity gives it sophistication, both here and in use.

OPPOSITE: Green isn't always an easy color to manipulate indoors. Breaking up surfaces and employing a number of different greens together helps. This is what designer Lisa Stafford and her husband, horticulturist Patrick Shaw, have done to their home in the Otway Ranges, west of Melbourne.

VIEW THIS PALETTE WITH THE GRAY VIEWER

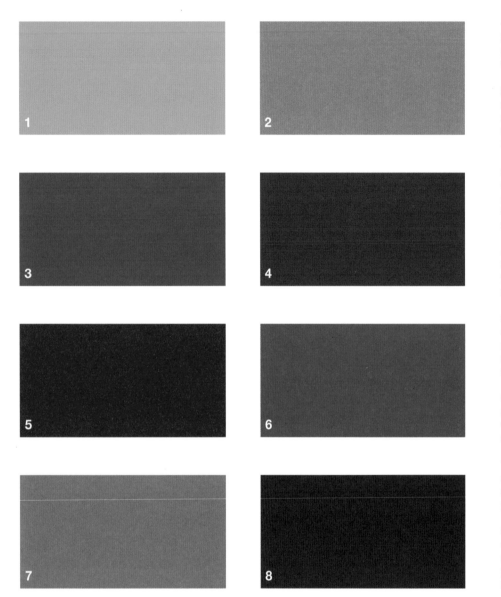

1 A good dirty mustard that was probably once brighter and more lemon-colored. Moving toward greenish brown. A standard shade in the Shaker furniture reproduction market.

2 A color of raw umber, a stock-in-trade antiquing color suggestive of general dirt. An excellent cool brown glazing color for wiping, stippling, or varnishing over paintwork to instantly add 200 years. Use with the yellow to lift its character.

3 Historically, cheap red paints were based on iron oxide (hematite). This is a typical example of the pigment's color: warm and brownish, the color of Shaker, Suffolk, and Swedish houses. This is not so much an ancient color as a timeless color.

4 A cooler, deeper, and more bluish version of color 3, and perhaps a dirtier one too. A color often used for early painted furniture, especially tables and chairs. Use with the darker colors below.

5 Grubby blues tend to green with the yellowing effect of dirt and nicotine, and very often paints made with Prussian blue pigment will take on a green cast. Another excellent early furniture color, often paired with polished wood.

6 The color of mid-blue paint that has taken on a surface bloom of white to render it almost gray. A very subtle color with traces of brown and green, and a smoky quality.

7 Just as blues turn greener with nicotine and age, so greens turn yellower. This is actually a very subtle color, but still with strength and character. View it as part of a palette with colors 5, 6, and 8 only.

8 Dark and dirty, a green that is a standard component of any historic paint range. A contender for eighteenth-century "Invisible Green" used to paint railings in front of foliage and pleasingly unsynthetic. Try it with the top two colors.

everal paint manufacturers sell deliberately "dirty" or "aged" paint colors as "pseudo-historic" colors. Others produce "heritage" ranges. They all use the same idea in their production: they add brown pigment to the color to dirty it. Some might add a touch of a color's complementary—a much more subtle touch and one that produces a color that is complex rather than just grubby. The colors here represent both those techniques.

By comparing this palette against colors from, say, the seventeenth to nineteenth centuries (see palette 17), you can see that these attempts are often pretty hopeless: colors in period decoration were in fact often very bright and clean; it's usually centuries of smut and nicotine that produce the tones that are then copied and marketed as "authentic" period colors.

But if you're painting a reproduction chair and you want to suggest that it's a 200-year-old Shaker or Pennsylvania Dutch piece, then these are perhaps the colors for you. They're the colors of theatrical fakery and of instant heritage.

VIEW THIS PALETTE WITH THE GRAY VIEWER

OPPOSITE: Putting a new and reproduction piece of furniture in an ancient setting can be an uncomfortable experience. Occasionally a mock heritage paint color can be invaluable.

Some of the most powerful and universal palettes are based on geology: on the colors of clays, of baked earth, of the desert, of rock, of earth pigments. This isn't at all surprizing, given that they all depend on the most common of all naturally occurring colorants, iron oxides. This palette demonstrates a range of colors that can be procured by cooking clay and consequently cooking the iron oxides inside the clay. It is based on typical ancient Greek pottery and so carries with it another associative value, that of the ancient world. It also appears in early nineteenth-century Greek revivalism as a base palette for late nineteenth-century polychromy and in Greek-inspired interiors from the 1930s.

1 A good deep terra-cotta, redolent of the detail work on ancient Greek pottery. Particularly vibrant with the plum color, below and to the right, since they are tonally equivalent.

2 A good warm iron oxide color with an orangeish undertone. Looks good and rich against black. This kind of warm red was prized in the past as an outdoor paint color.

3 Black, a dominant glaze color on Greek pottery, often used for background and line work.

4 A paler terra-cotta more suitable for larger areas.

5 A grayish, brownish plum: a bruised and complex color that hovers on the red side of

purple. This is a beautiful cusp color that will markedly change character according to the prevailing light.

6 Cream detail and panels (and later, backgrounds) occasionally surface on Greek pottery. As part of the entire palette, it is a highlight color to be used with restraint.

VIEW THIS PALETTE WITH THE BLACK VIEWER

ABOVE: This palette is very easy to assimilate because the colors are all so approachable and because they're so similar to the colors of other natural materials: stone, pottery, marble, and even wood, used here in the expert hands of designer Paul Daly.

1 An icy off-white that sharpens up every other color in this palette, especially the darker colors such as the red below.

2 An intense milky violet-blue. Can be used abundantly with the other three colors in this column.

3 A warm iron red. This color and the turquoise are the "outsiders" of this palette.

4 Almost ultramarine, this blue is produced in ceramics with cobalt compounds.

5 The red and this turquoise produce a shimmering effect when placed together because they are optical complementary colors. Try looking at this palette with just the red or just the turquoise.

6 This green has an anchoring effect on the red and turquoise. It can be used to great effect even in small quantities.

7 Tonally similar in value to the paler blue above. These two colors parenthesize the more strident dark colors in between. Obscure the two colors to the left to see how this works.

OPPOSITE: This palette may be determined by the available glaze colors that potters could historically use, but it has spread beyond ceramics and found use in paint and fabric all over the Middle East. Stephen Skinner's house in Marrakesh.

P erhaps it is the turquoise and sea green in this palette, perhaps it is the general predominance of blues and greens or the general cleanness of these colors, but this arrangement seems very clear and fresh, like the Aegean Sea. Of course colors have all sorts of emotional power and effects. Blue, particularly pale blues, are apparently calming; they certainly recede and so a blue room will appear to be larger than it is. Green is supposedly the color of balance and refreshment. Nero is said to have once appeared entirely clothed in green on the floor of the Coliseum, which itself was covered in green chrysocolla pigment, all in an attempt to rejuvenate both himself and his reputation.

The red and the turquoise are the two mavericks here and both can probably be used in minute squirts to spice up the other colors. All are in fact taken from Middle Eastern (mainly Turkish) tiles. These ceramics can be distinguished from their Oriental equivalents by the more liberal use of turquoise and green in their (basically blue) patterns.

Note that the red, although somewhat shaded, is the approximate complementary of the other colors, which make a broad band of blues and greens.

VIEW THIS PALETTE AGAINST WHITE

1 A good clean pale yellow ochre, which cheers up this entire palette. Very useful as a house color.

2 This purple-stained brownish gray is a pivotal color on this page. Try covering the lower half of this page and then add colors 9 and 10 of palette 37, overleaf, for a very subtle six-color palette.

3 An almost green-brown, useful for its ambiguity.

4 A dirtier and more restrained version of color 1.

5 This blue is slightly greenish and dirty, the color of a clear blue paint that has yellowed under varnish.

Delicate and very useable. A cusp color and therefore useful indoors.

6 A warm buff that is an essential component of this palette, as are all the neutrals. A good complex and ambiguous color.

7 A much warmer and less ambiguous color than color 6, but as a result of being pinker, it enlivens greens much better.

8 This deep olive intensifies the character of the palette on this page. Try obliterating it to see the difference. Use especially with the blue and ochres.

ABOVE: The advantage of working with a large palette of connected colors that have one coherent provenance is that it's not difficult to find objects and furnishings that fit into the overall scheme *somewhere*, such as in this room by New York-based architects Tsao & McKown. But with this kind of eclectic approach, it's important to get the objects together first, then paint the room in colors that will help "stitch together" the entire palette.

VIEW THIS PALETTE AGAINST WHITE OR WITH THE GRAY VIEWER

Here and on the next page is a collection of twenty colors that are all of a family. They have an earthy subtlety that suggests the palettes of North European cities. They could be the colors of Scandinavia or of American East Coast seaside houses. Their collective identity is strengthened by the suspicion that each color has something of all the others added to it.

Although they're different, there appears to be a common ancestry behind this entire palette, and this phenomenon will ensure that any combination of colors that you choose from this palette will work well together.

1 A warm, slightly brown off-white. Particularly good against the reds and pinks in this palette or the greens in palette 36.

2 The darkest color in this palette, but one that can be used to great effect to "point up" a combination of other colors, a trick that occurs in many mosaics.

3 A good warm neutral mid-gray. An invaluable color, not least because it suggests fur or suede.

4 A slightly more yellowish off-white. Use with yellows, reds, and pinks in this palette, and especially the blues in palette 36.

The reason for these colors' common quality is that they are all derived from minerals. These are the colors of rocks and stone, colors that are never bright hues but that nevertheless represent every segment of the color wheel. In this case they also represent every corner of the Roman Empire, since they are taken from a number of Roman mosaics from around the Mediterranean. So these are also the colors of ancient floors.

VIEW THIS PALETTE AGAINST WHITE OR WITH THE GRAY VIEWER

5 The most neutral off-white in this palette and an excellent wall and ceiling color.

6 A very clean pinkish iron red. Try using it as part of this column only, and with the greens in palette 36. A cusp color.

7 A neutral gray.

8 An off-white veering toward buff. Its grayness keeps it neutral and interesting.

9 A cooler, greener version of color 8. Try using them together with reds or greens.

10 A soft stony pink that relates to all the other reds on these pages. Use it with the greenish neutrals—colors 9, left, and 12, below—or with the greens or blue in palette 36. A very beautiful color for interiors.

11 A brick red to use with the greens in palette 36.

12 A good brownish gray, the color of a gray made with raw umber and white. Very useable in all media because it suggests gray without looking bluish.

1 A delicate and subtle blue, which was a medieval Chinese ceramic color.

2 "Duck Egg", another export Chinese ceramic color. All the colors on this page represent glazes that were applied as single colors to very simple forms. This blue-green is very useable and is a cusp color, sitting on the edge of blue.

3 This brown is the key color to this palette. Remove it and all the other colors appear more bland. Even a small quantity of this color will enhance a combination of the others. Try it with any one of the others for a very robust relationship. From medieval Chinese bowls.

4 A robust and slightly dirty greenish cream, from a seventeenth-century teapot. Both the object and this color were copied in 1930s ceramics. Use the color as an "old" white.

5 An exquisite sage green, immediately suggestive of Chinese porcelain and a very subtle color. Try using it with just the other two colors in this column.

6 Another delicate color, very 1920s in feel (see also palette 19). Try using it with just the other two colors in this column.

Here are the colors of water and air pitched against those of chalk and earth. A very modern palette ideally suited to the New Modernist mantra of "light, space, and clarity". But like so many apparently up-to-the-minute palettes in this book, it is actually much, much older, and has its roots in ancient Chinese ceramics.

The trade routes to the Orient were opened up by the Dutch in the seventeenth century, but contact with Oriental culture was limited to a small number of designated ports. Consequently, both China and Japan quickly established manufacturing industries producing items specifically for export to the West that were made to cater for Western tastes, which means that since the early 1600s our understanding of Oriental color and design has always been controlled at the source. All the colors on this page are taken from Oriental ceramics (all of which are listed in the "Notes to the Palettes" section on page 180). The colors form a coherent palette redolent of the 1920s and even of nineteenth-century Orientalism (William Morris used this palette in his wallpapers).

VIEW THIS PALETTE WITH THE GRAY VIEWER

ABOVE: The aquatic and aerial connotations of this palette are brought out in this room through the use of materials (such as glazed tiles and glass) and by zoning the color so that blue is used only in the bathroom. Brown appears as dark wood, which connects to the other story here: the use of natural or simple materials such as wool and concrete.

simple palettes

1 "Aka", thought to be red, and the finest, "makka", is bright vermilion red. No holds barred.

2 White is "shiro" and at its finest, "masshiro".

3 Black is "kuro", and the purest pitch black, "makkuro".

4 Blue, "ao", is the fourth color and when refined, it is "massao", or sky blue. Only these four colors can be prefixed with the superlative "ma", meaning "true" or "perfect".

This is one of the few palettes in this book that represent a philosophy—here it's a set of ideas that underscore a culture, Japanese culture. It might have been possible to put together a palette representing the modern country, but the modern Japanese visual zeitgeist is now so Westernized and chromatically fractured that it is difficult to pull out of the wreckage of advertising and youth culture any coherent visual statement. So here instead are the colors of old Japan, which are still revered, used, and referred to daily. The four-color palette on this page represents a traditional decorative palette of refined pigments that were mentioned in the first Japanese history dating from the eighth century, have been formally codified through the centuries, and are still engrained in Japanese culture. Twelve centuries later, the four colors remain the basic structure on which Japanese color perception and nomenclature are based. They make one powerful palette.

VIEW THIS PALETTE WITH THE GRAY VIEWER

Luis Barragán, the Mexican architect, had an instinctive and unswerving understanding of color. His (possibly knowing) use of the Japanese primaries for the indoor pool at Casa Gilardi, Mexico City, in 1977 suggests a mastery of the physiological and associative effects of the colors. The cobalt blue obviously suggests, and connects to, the water. It also appears to recede slightly. The red on the other hand advances optically: the red wall looks as though it is disconnected from anything else and is marching out of the water.

ABOVE: When blocking color in a room, a common cheat is to find objects, such as this cushion, that pull all the colors together in one place. Of course, it's so much more clever to find a cushion you like and design the scheme around it. No one will know the difference.

Here's a palette that can hardly keep itself under control. Mercifully, a good dollop of brown brings it into order. But despite its recklessness, it has a venerable history. Until the twentieth century, our society's understanding of color was heavily dependent on the use and availability of pigments, dyes, and glazes that could be formulated, refined, and processed from naturally occurring materials. Reds were extremely difficult to procure: bright red pigment was highly prized, permanent dye almost impossible to achieve, and red glaze elusive (note the complete absence of red from palette 59). The Chinese and Japanese, however, successfully processed large quantities of red colorants for use in manuscript writing, lacquer work, silk dyeing, and ceramics. These three reds are, to an extent, the West's impression of Far Eastern culture. They are, if you like, "trademark" Oriental colors that have reached far into our collective cultural consciousness. As such, they are very powerful markers of all things Eastern. They're matched with an intense yellow, the color of dyed silk robes from all Chinese periods.

In palette 38 there are more trademark Oriental colors that are especially suggestive of the late nineteenth and early twentieth centuries. See also the Oriental ceramics palette 60, as well as palette 46 for more trademark export pinks and greens.

1 "Silk Red", a color achieved by intensive dyeing with madder. A warm orange-red of pure hue. Very appealing; a color that optically "advances" toward the viewer.

2 The color of Chinese lacquer. Although carved lacquer is derived from a tree resin, its typical red coloring is from the addition of cinnabar (mercuric sulfide) that was ground into the resin. Chinese vermilion pigment is synthetic cinnabar and is still exported. See also palettes 39 and 45 for vermilion matches from other sources. A beautiful rich red that sits between the hue, left, and red oxide.

3 "Oxblood", derived from a ceramic glaze developed in the early fifteenth century and improved in the seventeenth century into this color. The glaze was made with copper and was notoriously unreliable, so products glazed in red were therefore expensive. An eighteenth-century variant was "Peach Bloom", a mottled, more intense, and even pricier version. Brown was never more expensive.

4 Chinese yellow, an intense and warm color that is characteristic of robes of all periods.

VIEW THIS PALETTE AGAINST WHITE OR WITH THE GRAY VIEWER

This sitting room by Jonathan Reed plays a game with this palette, adopting the colors in tiny quantities and spattering them around the room in objects and furnishings. The variety of styles and textures adds to the pleasing complexity of this look.

41 gilt-edged, blue-blooded

1 A bright ochre-like yellow, but more vibrant, like a lead-tin yellow. A little milky and subdued and so very useable.

2 An equally milky tint of cobalt blue, pure, and untainted by either green or purple. Its strong relationship with the yellow derives from their shared restrained tonality against the black—and white of the page. That's a very refined relationship between them and one worth exploiting for its edgy balance.

3 A key color in this palette. Try looking at the blue and yellow through the gray viewer while covering the black. They need black and white to provide a resonating contrast.

This is one of those palettes of colors that repeatedly pops up its head through history. It is one persistent set of colors. The relationship of green to its complementary, red, is a dialogue that has been explored in every sphere of the pure and applied arts (see palettes 43, 44, 45, and 46). But this palette is far more particular and well-balanced: a neutral dusty cobalt gently complements a bright ochre tint. The three colors here, together with white, form part of the Minoan and early Greek palettes. They also appear in the early nineteenth century as English ceramic colors and in twentieth-century ceramics. They're the colors used in tile schemes in some Moroccan palaces and they're even similar to the muted primaries of 1950s lithographic printing (see palette 42). This may look like an innocent and anonymous team of colors, but it's actually a powerful combination.

VIEW THIS PALETTE AGAINST WHITE

Given the trickiness of this palette and its unusual provenance, you might think these colors have never been used for interior decoration. In fact, they crop up together quite a lot, perhaps because their muted grayness successfully joins together what otherwise would be a trio of strident primitive primaries.

I f these primary colors have a vintage feel, you've already been hooked: hooked by your memory onto the lure of the palette's origin. These are actually Egyptian colors of the fourteenth and fifteenth centuries B.C., but they're here principally because they are also colors of the 1950s and 1960s. However, these are not the colors of buildings or interiors of these two decades, nor of bright modernist furniture, nor even of fashion. These are the colors of how the times were communicated then. In an age of gray newsprint and of black-and-white TV, these are three colors from the world of glossy magazines, the swinging primaries of offset lithography. Of course, the basic ink colors of commercial lithographic printing are nothing like these colors (see color model 4 on page 11); these are the dull cousins of bright hues that offset lithography strives to produce through combinations achieved by layering inks. Forty years ago, these colors were often the best technology could achieve.

The red, yellow, and blue shown here are a tribute, not to 1950s and 1960s design, but to how it was seen by millions, and because of ink fading, how subsequent decades saw it. Interestingly, blackened colors such as these have recently been used to sell a reborn 1960s icon, the Mini Cooper.

1 A warm red formulated with an overprint of 20 per cent black (to give you an idea of its grubbiness). Because of this mix of grayness and warmth, this is actually a very approachable and useable red.

2 A complex yellow with 10 per cent black and 6 per cent orange to prevent it from turning green. Not strident, so good with the red or blue.

3 The intensity and permanence of Phthalocyanine pigment in cyan printing inks means this color is least affected by poor print quality, over-abundance of black and fading. Fifteen per cent black ensures this color is complex and interesting.

VIEW THIS PALETTE AGAINST WHITE OR WITH THE GRAY VIEWER

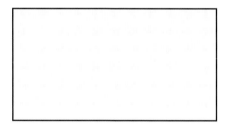

1 A deep "rosso" red. For those supercar buffs, "rosso" is simply the Italian word for "red". You could almost get away with painting your dining room this color.

2 A brighter red that contrasts vividly when set against the green, below. Since World War I, red has been the agreed international racing color of the Italians.

3 This green is almost black and is about as accurate a match as is possible to the chimerical "British Racing Green" or to be correct, "Napier Green". This was the racing color for British cars, although the greens actually used varied wildly.

4 Off-white or "Vintage White" seems to accompany many other colors and was the prewar German racing color. After the war the Germans raced in silver—or even bare polished metal—earning them the title "Silver Arrows".

This is the start of our red and green story, one of the greatest love affairs in the torrid history of color. But here they are paired almost accidently because this palette is based not on one object or place but on international racing car colors. Researching car colors is, on the whole, a waste of time. Manufacturers don't keep records of the colors they used fifty years ago; colors change at the whim of owners and factory owners; cars rust and their paint fades outdoors. Even Ferrari, which is famous for one color, has used possibly dozens of different reds over the years. However, there are scraps of scholarship available and I have listed a brief and interesting history of racing colors in the "Notes on the Palettes" section on pages 181–2. So this palette is an informed but still very personal selection: two sports car reds, one British Racing Green, one Vintage White. A small choice. Henry Ford would have cautiously approved.

OPPOSITE: David Carter is a designer who will never avoid an issue. In the home he shares with his wife, Lizzie, in London, he's grabbed this palette by one red horn and one green horn and given it a good kicking. He has made the scheme more pliable by underpainting the green with gold paint and by adding opulent 1930s and 1940s furnishings. This is an exciting and intriguing space.

VIEW THIS PALETTE WITH THE GRAY VIEWER

O f all the examples of red and green palettes that history has revealed, none is more agreeable than this one: magenta red and sage green. This is the palette of delicate nineteenth-century French printed linen and of chintz wallpaper. These colors date from the 1950s, the 1920s, and the eighteenth and nineteenth centuries. They are even medieval, for the simple reason that they represent common dyed fabric colors, those produced by woad and indigo for blue, by weld for yellow, and by roots from the madder plant, which yielded a range of intense pinks and reds.

But the earliest, most coherent use of red and green together occurs in seventeenth-century India, from where the fashion for this palette spread throughout Europe. These swatches were all matched against Murghal wall hangings and floor coverings, delicately embroidered with tracing floral patterns in fine, beautifully dyed silk that printing inks cannot hope to emulate.

If you are looking for any kind of balance or lightness of touch when using all these colors, it's essential that the magenta is used sparingly. The ground color should dominate or balance the green in quantity. The red and pink are secondary. Experiment by using the gray viewer and blocking out portions of the red and pink swatches.

Alternatively, use the green and the pink together freely.

1 A sage-like green but with more yellow in it. Similar to many "historic" green paint colors. The foliage color of Murghal hangings. Use in quantity against the red.

2 Neutral off-white ground color, very useful when juxtaposed against the red to control it and as a support for the green.

3 Magenta-red pink, but fairly deep. Can be used in abundant quantity with the green. These two colors together form a very flexible palette.

4 Deep magenta-red used with the pink as the floral color in Murghal hangings. Use with care.

5 Historically, green fabrics were produced by overdyeing a blue dye with a yellow dye, such as weld. As the yellow dye fades over time it reveals the soft blue of the woad or indigo used beneath. This color is a good foil to the pinks and greens of this palette.

6 This color is equivalent in tonality and intensity to the color. left, and can be used with it or with any combination of colors in this palette.

VIEW THIS PALETTE AGAINST WHITE

ABOVE: Although these colors can be used in blocks and large areas for big impact, they have traditionally been mixed in small patterns, following the early inspirations for the palette: roses and other wild flowers. Cath Kidston is the latest designer to rework this vocabulary.

1 and 2 This first pair of colors appeared together in 1350. Here the deep and blackened green has some blue in it. The red, equivalent to a slightly dull vermilion, is relatively pure. To avoid the green looking completely black, it should not be used as a detail color against the red but in large areas (see the photograph for palette 43). The red will support being used in small areas, but will appear to "hover" in front of the green.

3 and 4 The historical equivalent of orange is red lead. Its light tonal value contrasts starkly with the very dark green. This tonal contrast makes up for the fact that the hues of these two colors are not complementary on any color wheel but occupy the same third of the wheel. The result is that orange detail on a green ground will be clear and readable. But, as above, the dark green will appear black if the relationship is the other way around.

5 and 6 Color 5 is another intense red, brighter, and moving toward orange. This time the green in color 6 has given up; it's too weedy by comparison. The only way it can fight back is with volume, so a combination of these two colors must employ the red sparingly, otherwise the green will look gray.

The great dialogue between red and green is one of the major ideas running through the history of color. But there is a secondary, related idea about pinks and purples, and orange, and how, in the minds of artists, they have also been worthy adversaries of green.

The juxtaposition of a pure spectrum red with pure green to produce a shimmering complementary effect is not common before the twentieth century. The nearest thing occurs in medieval fashion, where different-colored robes were worn together (although the notion of the two colors as complementary did not emerge until much later). But what does occur a lot throughout history is the modification of one or both colors to a tint, or a darkened tone, or a grayed or otherwise muted color.

The references for the colors here come from Tuscan and Sienese Renaissance painted furniture, on which the interplay of red and green was experimented with for several hundred years.

Fashion designer Oswald Boateng has no qualms about using these two colors in the way they work best: in large expansive areas. Polished wood and other more patterned elements act as marriage brokers in the wild red/green relationship.

VIEW THIS PALETTE WITH THE GRAY VIEWER

1 A cool bluish mauve pink, which sharply contrasts with the acid green to the right to make a very exciting combination.

2 An intense sharp green, striking against most colors, especially purples.

3 A typical Sèvres pink, supposedly invented by Mme. du Pompadour and named after her, its name later changed to "Rose DuBarry". There is enough white here to make the color versatile, enough blue to prevent it from turning sugary.

4 A complementary green to the pink, left, representing "Sèvres Vert". Also tinted with white.

5 A generic intense pink that came to represent Sèvres "Famille Rose". Also the color of some early Dutch ceramics painted in imitation of imported Orientalware.

6 A Sèvres blue, a version of "Bleu Celeste", lightened with white to tonally balance the "Famille Vert" and "Famille Rose" colors.

OPPOSITE: You could get no more Sèvres than this: the restored apartments of Mme. du Pompadour (with silk curtains by Verel de Belval). The work was supervised by Pierre-Xavier Hans and Christian Baulez, curators of the Château de Versailles.

This palette continues—and develops—the honorable red-green dialogue. The bottom four colors on this page consist of pinks and softened greens that in the main are all shifting toward blue, giving them a collective family trait. The top pair, however, contrast more sharply with each other. Here, the pink is moving markedly to blue, while the green is moving to yellow, blue and yellow also being complementary. This is a complicated game they're playing.

This is a interesting since the top pair of colors is taken from a primary reference source—Chinese porcelain—while the other four indicate French eighteenth-century taste, being colors formulated in the Sèvres factory, which in the 1760s began to imitate Oriental imported ceramics to satisfy domestic demand. In any case, these colors mutated slowly through time: by the late nineteenth century the pinks (of the Harewood bottle, made in imitation of Sèvres) had become warmer and a little sickly.

VIEW THIS PALETTE AGAINST WHITE

LEFT: The objects from which this palette came are weavings from Iceland. This historic interior from the 1880s is also Scandinavian. It is the artists Carl and Karin Larsson's house, Lilla Hyttnäs, in Sweden.

1 This is the color of yellow ochre mixed with white, an earthy yellow. Good for decoration.

2 A light Brunswick green, a color much used for exterior house painting in the nineteenth century and employed as a standard color in many international color systems since the 1900s.

3 This is a slight tint of the best grade of orange vermilion pigment, in use throughout history as a rare and expensive color. The most important color in this palette, even when used sparingly.

4 The ambiguity of this color makes it fascinating to look at, especially when surrounded by other colors. Producible as a paint by mixing Prussian blue (available cheaply from the early 1700s) and yellow ochre, and popular in many countries as a furniture color from the eighteenth century onward.

There is something very satisfying about this collection of four colors. They are certainly all "off" in one way or another: the red is pale, burnt, and slightly orange, the color of baked bean sauce; the yellow is straw colored; the green is yellowed and dark; and the blue is actually deep turquoise. On reflection, these are of course versions of the four color primaries—red, yellow, blue, and green—an obvious starting point for a palette. And yet, these colors are not discrete, they subtly interpenetrate each other: the red, it seems, has been weakened by the addition of the yellow; the blue has been polluted by the green, the green by the yellow, and the yellow by a mixture of them all. The key to a successful color grouping is often a clever admixture of the colors between themselves, something that has happened here.

The sources for this palette are seventeenth-century weavings from the then-relatively isolated culture of Iceland. The patterns are simple and the colors distinct: those of wool dyed with the most common dyes derived from lichens, or plants such as woad. The colors are also representative of four important historic pigments.

VIEW THIS PALETTE WITH THE GRAY VIEWER

ABOVE: Colors are never of themselves "historical", they are just colors; but when used together they can nevertheless suggest a connection to ancient things. This apartment in Anvers, France, which belongs to the architect Jo Crepain, demonstrates that point. The palette's primitiveness imbues the place with a sense of timelessness and immutable permanence.

1 This dusty red has all the qualities of a good hematite red oxide. Try it paired with the blue.

2 A deep green-gray, almost black, the color of linework in Minoan painting. En masse, this color also works well with the blue, or with the yellow.

3 A chalky off-white with a pink cast, the color of wet gypsum.

4 This delicate pale cobalt blue is sufficiently strong to contend with the other three major colors. Compare it and the two other colors in this column with palette 41. A beautiful and useable color.

5 An intense golden yellow, almost too strong to be an ochre, but a useful detail color against any of the other colors, particuarly the near-black and the blue.

This is a well-balanced palette where the colors appear to have a dusty film over them. This reticence renders them ideal for decoration or use in large areas because the dusty finish "knocks" the colors back into the wall. The colors are in fact very ancient. In the quest for the earliest known palette of colors, the Egyptians run a close second since they used a complex set of pigments from the earliest times. But the first artists were cave dwellers and the most primitive hand stencils found in French caves were achieved with red- and ochre-colored earths, and soot or charcoal from their fires. Their four colors—the off-white stone background, yellow, red, and black—are still being used by Aboriginal artists.

The palette here marks a step forward and dominated Mediterranean wall painting for almost a thousand years. It originated in Crete and represents the colors of Minoan muralists of the fifteenth and sixteenth centuries B.C. The colors were still being used together in third-century B.C. Etruscan frescoes. The red is good and pure, the yellow is bright, and there is a soft blue. The Minoans traded vigorously around the Mediterranean and would have culled their materials and pigments from far and wide. Equally, they profoundly influenced other societies, from which it is possible to deduce that these are also the colors of pre-classical Greece. In fact, this palette does occur on the Greek mainland from the thirteenth century B.C. onward.

VIEW THIS PALETTE AGAINST WHITE OR WITH THE GRAY VIEWER

There is an earthy cheerfulness about this palette, perhaps because these are the colors of rock, sand, and sky; perhaps because these are organic versions of childlike primaries—red, yellow, blue, and black—only green is missing.

But since the complementary of cyan blue is yellow (warm yellow in the four-color palette and pure yellow among the optical primaries and secondaries—see the color models on pages 8–11) there ought to be more of a struggle going on here. One reason why there isn't may have something to do with this palette's origin. These are not only the colors of a hot country's landscape; they are also the colors of mineral pigments that have been in use for thousands of years, so we're subconsciously very familiar with them.

This is a palette of our cultural ancestors: the Minoans and Greeks used it as their essential basic palette (see palette 48), the Romans adopted it, and it was among the colors of Native Americans. However, the plenteous use of the intense blues shown here is particularly indicative of early Mayan wall paintings, the source for these colors.

1 A good orange-tinged earth red. The color of good-quality iron oxide pigment.

2 The intense blue of "Maya blue"—a pigment made with indigo. Obliterate the red to see how this color works well with the black and yellow (see also palette 41).

3 The color of yellow ochre, sister to the red, above. Its strength and depth of tone (as against bright primary yellow) means it has an equable relationship with the black. For a different blue/black/yellow relationship, compare this with palette 41.

4 A useable clear tint of the blue, above. Try it with just the red or just the yellow and black.

5 Black is used as the line color in many early wall paintings and is a key contributor to many palettes based on mineral pigments.

VIEW THIS PALETTE AGAINST WHITE

Mayan it may not be, but it's on the same continent: a bedroom from the 1950s-inspired hotel Boquitas Pintadas in Buenos Aires. The 1950s saw the adoption of classical and ancient color schemes into contemporary fabric and product design.

complex palettes

ABOVE: The English home of potter and artist Rupert Spira is a masterly exercise in the manipulation of light with color. His decorating palette consists almost entirely of traditional pigments.

1 A warm chalky off-white that can look cream under intense lighting. Suitable as an exterior off-white. Formulated with white, raw umber, and yellow ochre.

2 The color of backlit plain porcelain and rice pudding. A difficult color due to its orange warmth, but useful. A good foil to many of the greens and blues in this palette and a much-used exterior color.

3 A pink that despite its apparent sugariness has an historic place in decoration. Works well with ceramic blues and will change color according to lighting due to the blue undertone it has. The color of my dining room.

4 Part of a fashionable group of colors that contain violet, gray, and brown, this one is another cusp color that will change markedly under different lighting conditions. Use with cream or white.

ABOVE: Just because colors work well in old houses, it doesn't mean they can't be used in a contemporary setting, or for that matter somewhere other than a northern climate. The architect Bert Pepler dipped into this palette for his house in Kalk Bay, South Africa.

Brighter, equatorial, and tropical colors can look tired and inappropriate out of context. In climates where the sky is predominantly cloudy and particularly where that cloud is thick and low (such as the UK, Netherlands, and parts of North America) full-spectrum daylight is filtered. Clouds allow the blue end of the spectrum to pass unhindered while blocking substantial amounts of the red and orange end, resulting in what we call a "gray day", lit by blue-tinted light. This "Northern Light" palette was formulated to combat that. The yellows, pinks, and reds are all formulated as complex pigments (in paints these are earth pigments such as yellow and red ochres) that dodge the blue light.

As a result, creams made with yellow ochre, for example, will not turn greenish, even in a north-facing room. There are additional blues and greens that take subtle and complex advantage of a predominantly blue-light spectrum.

VIEW THIS PALETTE AGAINST WHITE OR WITH THE GRAY VIEWER

5 An ideal cream that in paint form is matched by a mixture of white and yellow ochre only. This is a cream that refuses to look cold or greenish under any natural lighting condition.

6 A yellow made up with yellow ochre only, a complex, muddy pigment that ensures that under poor and cool lighting conditions the color will veer toward brown rather than green.

7 A good cool neutral stone color. Made with raw umber and white pigments.

8 This deeper warm gray is the color of old oak when left outside.

9 One of the prettiest and most innocent colors

I have ever used. Very approachable and quite guileless.

10 A muddier tone of color 9 but still very useable.

11 A deeper cream, more tolerant in brighter lighting conditions, with more red in it. Suggestive of paints formulated with earth pigments.

12 A deeper yellow, tolerant of extreme lighting conditions and suggestive of place and historical uses, principally Italy.

13 An interesting and complex green with a slight oiliness. Good outdoors.

14 Another stone color, a tint of color 8. Together

with color 7 it forms a phalanx of neutral tints that will take on any other color here.

15 A more complex and slightly toned version of color 10. Good outdoors.

16 A deep outdoor blue. Use it as a detail color as part of the six top colors on this page (obscure the lower half to see the full effect).

17 Sand color, again matched to earth-pigmented paint, containing iron oxides that themselves are the true coloring material of sands and rocks.

18 A golden ochre tint. Use with other colors in the two left-hand columns or for greater effect with just colors 17, 23, and 24.

8

9

10

14

15

16

20

21

22

26

27

28

19 This is a delightful and slightly blued green, clean and clear. It works as part of the larger group of greens here and can be used with any or all of them.

20 A slightly more traditional decorating green, subtle and grayed. The most useable decorating green here.

21 A beautiful and purple-tinged blue made by adding ultramarine blue pigment to white. The color of my bedroom and a tint that appears to alter character through the day as the light changes.

22 A deeper tint of color 21, better suited to outdoors.

23 An earthy sand color, again formulated with earth (clay) pigments.

24 Terra-cotta comes in a wide range of colors. This one is intended to match lighter-colored pottery and is a warm pinky brown formulated from the same earth pigments that color the ceramic clay.

25 The red of a traditionally decorated dining room or picture gallery, being a lighter and interior version of color 26. Just the right tint for indoors.

26 From Morocco to northern France, Norway to America, traditional (especially wooden) buildings have been painted in reds such as this, made from

hematite (iron oxide). This version is warm, uncompromising and cheerful.

27 A pretty but uncompromising sage green with enough blue in it to alter character under different lighting conditions (and therefore a cusp color).

28 Another uncompromising bluish green but one with hairs on its chest. Assertive and good outdoors.

**VIEW THIS PALETTE AGAINST WHITE OR
WITH THE GRAY VIEWER**

The apartment of Cape art dealer Michael Stevenson is a latter-day version of Mme. Récamier's room: soft and curving but a carefully controlled statement.

Many of the palettes in this book are derived from particular objects or schemes that are representative of an era or place, but they can only tell a tiny part of a much bigger story. I'm aware of the danger in choosing them as ambassadors of a bigger and more complex idea. It's impossible, for example, to represent every color of the eighteenth century, or to show one room that in some way is the acme of the period. For this reason, I've often resorted to showing groups of colors from several sources together—or even collating the work of other researchers to give a more comprehensive palette.

But here I've been able to rely on one source with reasonable trust. These colors are taken from a watercolor of about 1802 of the bedchamber of Mme. Récamier, the wife of a wealthy Parisian banker who had his house redecorated by the designer Berthault in 1798. The scheme represents what was then the very latest in fashionable taste: a combined Roman/Greek-style interior hung with silk and furnished with reproduction classical bronze artifacts. The house was visited by anyone interested in this new style and became an influential example of what was to become French Empire style. This palette stands out as an exemplary combination of delicately balanced colors.

1 The violet color of Mme Récamier's wall hangings, and no doubt an intoxicating color when dyed onto silk. Very useable, especially with the cream or with white.

2 This cream is just slightly orange-tinged. Use with the violet or just with the pink for a more rustic early twentieth-century scheme.

3 A cool bluish pink, the color of a tint of Indian red. A cusp color, like the violet: used together they make a color scheme that is very sensitive to changes in light.

4 This reddish brown is the color of the furniture in the Récamier room and should be used with discretion in this palette. Alternatively, use it as the main color. Compare these four colors to the first four of the Northern Light palette.

VIEW THIS PALETTE AGAINST WHITE

This palette grows out of the two preceding it. It plays around with reds and oranges, chooses a neutral, and then crafts them into an exquisite blend with a delicate lilac and a totally clean blue. The key colors here are actually the brown and purple. Both help anchor the entire palette and give it fiber. The purple is delicately phrased (as is so often the case).

But for spark, nothing comes close to the blue. Without it, the palette dies. Its cool presence makes for a very sophisticated combination that is very appealing to the modern eye, although in fact many of these colors were used together in early nineteenth-century fabrics and wallpapers.

1 A good picture room red, deep and bruised. It has a bluish bias and is an uncompromising color. Note how the three reds have different characters but get on with one another.

2 A rusty orange that pairs well with color 1 because they are almost equally intense, from a similar part of the spectrum but of different perceived temperatures: whereas the red is dark and cold, this is bright and warm.

3 The third player from the same part of the spectrum, but its dusty character renders it more useable and softer in character than color 1. Use it with the blue and the two colors below.

4 A suspiciously cheerful blue, but one with a slightly icy smile. A cool toothpaste color that needs the other colors in this palette to bring it to life.

5 A very subtle violet that acts as a bridge between the blue and the other colors here. Try covering it up to see how this works.

6 Sludge: bluish green-gray. Not an obvious first choice for many people, but umber-based browns like this are invaluable "rooting" colors in many schemes.

An eclectic palette such as this suits an eclectic scheme. This apartment in Sydney, designed by Tim Janenko Panaeff, is a funky mix of twentieth-century chic: Eames chairs, a Danish 1960s coffee table, and modern rugs. The look plays with different earthy reds that are all tied together with a dash of pale blue.

VIEW THIS PALETTE AGAINST WHITE

1 A clear yellow ochre cream free of any hint of dirtiness. Rich and warm, a color that will work as a background/backbone to any other combination from this palette.

2 An earthy pink the color of city walls in Jaipur, Essaouira, and Taroudant. A cool pink with no trace of delicacy or the synthetic. So a macho color.

3 Deeper sandier ochre, from which the tint above comes. Use it as a key color, with only the four colors in this column or the four in the central section of these eight.

4 A right-in-the-face iron hematite red. Bluish and dusty, a very common color worldwide. Use with the other three colors at the top of this page.

5 A tint of ultramarine blue and hence tending to purple. Also a good indigo dye blue. A very persistent color that maintains its "color constancy" regardless of which other colors it is placed against. Use with the three other colors in this central section or as part of a four-color palette using the lower four colors (obscure the other colors with your hand to see how the intensity of this color does not change).

6 Dust color, from the Thar Desert, Saharan city walls, and parched Mediterranean coast. This color appears in local sands and clays and consequently in building cements, mortars and plasters. A good warm neutral buff color to use especially with the ochres, above, or the greens, below.

7 This malachite green is dusty and grayed, the color of worn painted doors and decorative detail. Pair it with the blue above for a dynamic combination.

8 A slightly milky vivid tint that hovers between turquoise blue and green. It's the color of verdigris on copper or bronze and also the color of paint made with that mineral.

Travel leaves the colors of exotic destinations printed on our memory like a stain of the place itself. Some places have particularly strong palettes and originally I thought of assembling separate palettes for North Africa, the Mediterranean, and the Indian subcontinent. But these seemed ridiculously large geographical areas to try to sum up with just half a dozen colors for each. Anyway, there are, without doubt, countless palettes with which tribes, villages, and cities brand themselves individually. So I scrapped the idea. But in looking at the generalities of architectural color across these vast landmasses, similarities and coincidences began to occur that were too interesting not to record. So here is a palette of much more general colors that belong to those three hot, dry climates. There are the blues of Sahrouis costume, Marrakesh, and villages in Greece; the ochres and sand colors of the Sahara and Thar Deserts; the copper-based bluish green paints that pop up regularly in Morocco, India, and Greece; and the earth pinks of the walls of Jaipur and Essaouira. These building colors are representatives of these places: the palette, if anything, is a shortcut to the character of a swathe of culture, that run from the Atlantic to the Indian Oceans.

VIEW THIS PALETTE AGAINST WHITE OR WITH THE GRAY VIEWER

The traditional and tribal languages of color can be lifted and dropped right into a modern scheme. This New York loft connects straight to this palette with commissioned perspex screens, furniture by Eames and Bertoia, and ceramics by Russell Wright.

BELOW: These colors are of course not restricted to desert regions. This is a guest room from Ekshäradsgården, a Scandinavian manor house.

OPPOSITE: The places where you will find deep ultramarine blue or indigo used with abandon are in the streets of Greece, on Indian walls, and in the houses of Morocco. This is the home of Françoise Dorget (creator of the shop Caravane) and the architect Charles Chauliaguet near Tangiers.

Blue is a color that, like a rare spice, follows a trail from exotic countries to the Mediterranean. These particular blues can now be produced by universal colorants, but they began their journeys in Africa and India.

Indigo, as the name suggests, was being exported from the Indes in Pliny's time during the Roman Empire and remained the primary source of blue dye in the Middle East until synthetic indigo was isolated in the late nineteenth century (natural indigo's equivalent in Europe was woad). It was also added to paint as a pigment (as at Jodhpur). Ultramarine blue pigment, sourced originally by the Oxus River in Afghanistan, was being refined from lapis lazuli as an intense deep blue sometime during the eleventh to twelfth centuries. From there it found popular appeal all over the known world, to be then synthesized in the 1800s in France. Its antecedents, azurite blue and Egyptian blue, were in use in Egypt millennia before, as were cobalt blue and copper blue glass (from which Egyptian blue was made). Recently, the artist Yves Klein developed a number of synthetic ultramarine variants, including a blue bearing his name, "International Klein Blue". The architect and artist Louis Majorelle famously used a similar ultramarine, now known as "Bleu Majorelle", in his garden in Marrakesh in 1924, which was recently restored by the fashion designer Yves Saint Laurent.

India and North Africa are the source of blue and still the home of blue.

OPPOSITE: Rupert Spira decorated his English home with many of the colors that occur in the Northern Light palette 50, but this room seems to take its inspiration from hotter countries. The shared natural sources of the colorants in both palettes means that they are entirely compatible.

VIEW THIS PALETTE AGAINST WHITE OR WITH THE GRAY VIEWER

9 A deep and impure woad or indigo blue, slightly grayed and purplish. Although deep, this is a delightful color that comes alive when used with the burnt orange, right.

10 Burnt orange, an earthy color. An unusual combination with the blue and the gray-violet, below.

11 Another ultramarine or indigo tint, warm and aerial, as if looking at a blue sky. Use with just the color above and below it for a wild blue palette like the one pictured on the previous page.

12 Cooler and more cobalt (pigment) based than the other blues in this palette. Especially good with the burnt orange, above. Perhaps a more appropriate color for azurite pigment.

13 Dusty ultramarine, lacking the overpowering intensity of color 16 and so more useable,

particularly when heightened with small quantities of the turquoise green below.

14 A very useable and complex violet with plenty of warm gray in it. Use as a major element with the other three colors in the central part of this palette or as a means of subjugating color 16, below.

15 The color of turquoise Middle Eastern pottery glazes and the only color on this page with a green bias, this slightly dusty tint is a relation of the copper greens on the previous pages. Avoid using it with color 10, or there again, exploit their difficult relationship! At source, in Indian and Morocco, this is a detail color used against expanses of color 16.

16 The color of cobalt glass (not pigment), indigo-dyed silk, or ultramarine blue pigment.

1 A dull purple, typical of the rarer iron oxide violets. Interesting because it is less depressive or threatening than the equivalent blue or red. It has a good relationship with the yellow below.

2 This warm brown is a clean, reddish color. It's a color that can be used to tone all the other colors in this palette, turning them toward itself and reducing the overall contrast of the palette.

3 A light ochre yellow. It has a powerful relationship with the purple and is related closely to the red and brown. By removing the yellow—or the purple—the character of this palette is destroyed.

4 Iron oxides produce a wide range of reds (see the bluish pink on the next page) but perhaps the most prized are those that sit at the meeting point of orange-red and brown. A color in use from antiquity to the modern day.

There are several palettes in this book in which brown is a pivotal color, where it assumes an anchoring role. There are also several palettes where, strangely, purple has a similar role. The interesting thing about this palette is that it contains both, and as a result, this combination of colors is rock solid.

All four are muted and are uncontentious, since they all come from the same side of the color circle. They are also connected, at least in the natural world, by a common provenance: iron. These are the colors that iron oxides, present in geology worldwide, produce in rocks, stone, marbles, clays, and sands. You will find them again in palette 31.

So it is not surprising that iron oxides color many of the buildings of the world, not least in out-of-the-way places—this very appealing combination comes from homes in Guatemala.

VIEW THIS PALETTE WITH THE GRAY VIEWER

This London house designed by David Mikhail demonstrates a very neat trick: how to incorporate strong deep color into a minimal white room.

ABOVE: Not that you'd have thought it possible to find a room painted in these colors, but here is an interior, not from Japan but from a cottage in Ireland. And, surprisingly, the color scheme, in all its madness, works.

For centuries, color in Japan has been developed and codified—through applied arts, costume, theater, and religion—to a level of ritualized sophistication that is beyond our comprehension in the West. Only in Japan can grass be green but a "go" traffic light be blue; such is the conceptual refinement of color language there.

The development of such distinctions was also due in part to dyeing technology: early Japanese dyers experimented with a wide range of plant extracts and the technique of "overdyeing" to achieve intermediary colors—a process viewed with immense suspicion in the West until the Renaissance (the Greco-Roman and later the Christian view was that mixing color represented interference with the divine order). The three-color palette on this page represents a very ritualized element of Japanese life: the Kabuki theater in the Edo period (seventeenth to nineteenth centuries). They are postulated colors, formulated from recipes for dyeing the theater curtain hung at the opening of every performance.

1 Green based on the color "moegi", that of "green tinged with the yellow of onion tops, then grayed like strongly brewed green tea." An intense and almost lime green.

2 The Kabuki theater brown was also very specific: tannin from the persimmon would produce an orange that was then subdued with red mixed with black. Clearly, mixing and overdyeing were acceptable techniques. The resulting color is unremarkable by itself, but it has a subtle relationship with the other two colors, particularly the green.

3 The Edo Kabuki black was apparently tinged with purple and blue, something easier to see on dyed cloth that has a sheen, than on the printed page.

1 A yellowish moss green, difficult to use without the brown or cream.

2 Less yellow and more blue in this color. Very good with the cream.

3 This cream is pale and cool. It can afford to be: the brown here is very assertive.

4 A rich reddish brown, the color of burnt umber. An ofent-used pivotal color.

Here is a very refined palette made up of four colors and therefore very useable in its entirety. It uses one key color, brown, to "anchor" the scheme: if you obscure it, it's easy to see how the overall character of the palette is changed, whereas any other color can be dropped with little effect. It's interesting to note that brown often occurs as a pivotal color in a palette: its effect is profound and its presence often more important than black.

The colors have been taken from a 1920s Art Deco interior design scheme by the French firm Süe et Mare, and they are not controversial. There is, for example, no clash of similarly strident hues, although the reddish brown and dirty greens are vaguely complementary. But there is a structural relationship at work here that can often be found repeated in other schemes of the period: the use of two muted colors (here green) that are related (one lighter, one darker) set against a cream and a brown of some kind. It would be interesting to pursue this structure using different pairs of colors, with cream and brown, to see if the results all look equally Art Deco in spirit.

VIEW THIS PALETTE WITH THE GRAY VIEWER

Not a 1930s apartment at all but a brand-new one in London, built by Richard Rogers and decorated by Jonathan Reed.

ABOVE: The designer Philip Hooper is a master of the understated color blend. At his own seaside retreat
he has woven color stories through the space, taking a sophisticated color palette such as this one and
breaking it down into many small elements. It's a 1958 house, by the sea, on stilts. It's just waiting for a
VW Combi with surfboard attached. . . .

1 A glossy cherry red/red oxide mix called "Chianti Red" that looks its best when matched with white. All these four colors appeared on early Volkswagen Combis—and "Microbuses", as the manufacturer called them.

2 A deep sienna/ochre, "Sierra Yellow" that, because of its depth, looks particularly rich in gloss.

3 An iconic 1970s color for an iconic vehicle, burnt orange. Note how all these colors are "browned" to make them more interesting.

4 "Niagara Blue", the most restrained color in this collection of four, but interesting and still, like the others, very useable.

The colors of the millennium were bright and breezy. They came from palette 62. Those of the first decade of the twenty-first century are far more subdued and retrospective. The bright chromatic optimism of the late 1990s seems to be giving way to a more complex and restrained taste for muted colors, browns, burnt oranges, and the colors of the 1940s, 1950s and 1960s (see palettes 20, 21, 22, 23, and 24). These colors fit right into that taste, mainly because they are associated with a particular kind of mid-twentieth-century icon, the Volkswagen Combi.

VIEW THIS PALETTE AGAINST WHITE

1 Muddy turquoise. A complex and useful tone. Try hiding this color to radically alter the character of this palette.

2 A mix of the colors above and below. Hide this color to alter the balance of the palette.

3 A mix of the colors above and below. Cover this color to alter the balance of the palette.

4 Muddy orange, like a deep, rich ochre. Try hiding this color to radically alter the character of this palette.

This palette is representative of the kind of color play that some graphic artists and designers are now using. It might be hard to spot the formula at work behind these colors, but it is very simple: this palette is a journey between the color at the top and that at the bottom. Were there more swatches, the journey would be more obvious; the colors would appear to blend more easily into each other. But the palette becomes much subtler when just a few colors are picked out from that journey.

This is how it works: the blue at the top and the yellow at the bottom are of approximate equal luminous intensity and equally milky. They are impure tints of two hues, turquoise and orange, which appear directly opposite each other on modern color wheels that take four, rather than three, colors as their primaries and that, as a result, alter the relationships of those colors (see the color models on pages 8–11).

If you travel across the color wheel from one hue to another, bang in the middle you hit gray. But if those colors are not pure hues but muddied tints, like these, the middle ground between them will also be muddied and impure—as here.

OPPOSITE: This scheme, in Courtney Sloane's house, follows this palette's idea. Even the picture contributes (the reflections in the water providing the intermediary color steps).

VIEW THIS PALETTE AGAINST WHITE OR WITH THE BLACK OR GRAY VIEWER

ABOVE: As is so often the case, purple is the key anchoring color in this palette. The owners of this small hotel on the island of Rhodes obviously knew that.

1 A good neutral off-white-to-stone color approximating that found in the background glaze.

2 A tint of the same color. A pure white against the colors opposite will sharpen and crisp them. Use of these off-whites will quiet their effect and homogenize them into the kind of balanced arrangement that the Della Robbias achieved so well.

This combination of vibrant milky colors is taken from glazed terra-cotta ware of late sixteenth- and early seventeenth-century Florence, made by the Della Robbia family. The colors are striking for their family resemblance: optically, they each contain about the same amount of hue color and the same amount of black and white; there's not one that jumps out as being too intense. Consequently, they can all be used successfully together in virtually any combination. Their light tonality (the milky quality) occurs because of the quantity of white used. In a shiny coating, such as gloss, the milkiness would be retained. In a matt coating, such as emulsion, it would translate as a chalky dustiness.

3 All these greens have a large quantity of blue in them that contrasts vividly against the very warm yellow used. The yellow and green are as far away as possible from each other on the color wheel.

4 The nearest color to red that the Della Robbias achieved.

5 A delicate grass green that seems like a mix of several colors. Interesting and useable—although intense.

6 This blue is cooled somewhat by its gray content, but it sits chromatically around pure spectrum blue. Similar to Oriental ceramics blues.

7 An emerald green saved from uselessness by the thin veil of white or cream that appears to hover in front of it. A rich appley green that could work well outdoors.

8 A more useable tint of color 6, although it has a steely edge. A good balance for color 7 and particularly fine when used with colors 3 and 5.

9 The typical golden yellow of the Della Robbias and often contrasted against pale blue or green. Open and guileless, the color of sunshine or butter, but be warned: it can appear overpowering when used in large quantities. Moderate it with colors 3, 4, 5, or 10.

10 Probably the most approachable color here, but despite its dustiness, still assertive. Similar to a woad or indigo color.

The inclusion of colors in this palette that are in turn intense, bright, deep, dull, pale, and mid-toned makes for a subtle and complex whole: it is possible to choose virtually any combination of colors here. But the key colors are the turquoise and magenta. They are optical secondary colors that, like yellow, excite many more cones in the retina than reds, greens, or blues. Their role here is to point up the blues, but in this they are aided and abetted by the warm brown and the dull greens below.

The source for this palette is a variety of early Chinese and Japanese ceramics. The colors of willow pattern are here (colors 11, 12, 13, and 14), together with a variety of blues produced from cobalt glaze. The most interesting group is colors 3, 4, 5, and 6, which come from a Chinese alcohol jar on which they were arranged in a simple, abstract—and very modern—way.

1 A key color in this palette, strident against the deep blues, interesting in small quantities, especially against the pale blues and more neutral colors here.

2 The kind of deep ultramarine blue that cobalt glazes produce, a color at the core of Oriental ceramics.

3 A powerful green-blue-gray, a cusp color that will alter character under different lighting conditions.

4 A pinky brown of similar intensity (saturation) and tonality to colors 3 and 6. A cusp color.

5 A very purplish blue. Use as a line or accent color with the three colors around it.

6 The partner of color 3, above left. Subtle and grayish. A cusp color.

VIEW THIS PALETTE AGAINST WHITE

7 An icy pale blue that provides a background for color 8, right.

8 An intense bright and warm blue that resembles the pigment ultramarine. Use a neutral color to quiet it.

9 A slightly dirty and deep magenta. It can be used as the dominant color in a scheme with the neutral colors, left, and/or the pale blues. Or use it as a detail color to "spike" the deeper blues.

10 One of the deeper colors of Oriental ceramics, useful as a quiet line color with the four blues below.

11, 12, 13, and 14 These last four colors all derive from one type of Japanese pottery. Because they are all muted, slightly grayed versions of the other blues on this page (due to the impurity and firing temperature of the cobalt glaze on the original objects), they are very useable and work well together. For a very interesting and subtle palette, block out the top of the page and view these four with only the four lower ones opposite.

ABOVE: The Oriental ceramic palette plays through the purple-blue-green part of the spectrum, but both the purple and green veer toward blue. This Welsh home does the same thing. The pinky-brown painting works like color 4 on the previous page.

ABOVE: Another, purer example of mixing blue, brown, and a little pink (note the magenta-colored tulip and the bronze-pink of the sofa mattress). The work of the designer David Collins.

vibrant palettes

1 This is mauve. Not the washed-out color we now think of, but the dye first synthesized by scientist William Henry Perkins in 1856 and that launched the famous "Mauve Decade" in fashion. A fabulous color on silk or wool and a satisfying cross between purple and magenta.

2 Fuchsin, or magenta, so-named after the Battle of Magenta (the Italian city where the Austrians were defeated by the French and Sardinians in 1859). An extraordinarily powerful color with great optical properties. This example is closer to the nineteenth-century synthetic dye than the modern printing ink.

3 A beautiful crimson—a slightly bluish red—with depth and character. An approximation of alizarin crimson first synthesized in 1868. Try looking at it with just color 4.

4 Methyl violet, another early dye color that is purple without seeming cloying or opaque. Instead it seems positive and engaging. The dye still sometimes used to color methylated spirits.

These four colors make an intense, almost psychedelic palette that is on the one hand very typical of dyed sari silk and on the other typically groovy 1970s—the sort of colors that Danish designer Verner Panton used. They all have a slightly bluish tinge that connects them. They also belong in one part of the color wheel, that area between purple and red where magenta dominates. Because magenta is an optical secondary color—stimulating many more color receptors in the eye than a primary color—all these hues have an exciting luminous quality. They can all be used together.

In fact, the colors all derive from early synthetic dye technology of the 1850s and 1860s, a revolutionary time in the history of color that kick-started modern colorant production. Without it, modern Indian saris and Verner Panton interiors wouldn't be the same.

OPPOSITE: Here are some vibrant silks from Gujarat, hanging in Jaouad Kadiri's Marrakesh home built by architect Stuart Church. Nowadays, fabrics all over the world are dyed using lightfast and colorfast descendants of Perkins's early synthetic dyes.

VIEW THIS PALETTE AGAINST WHITE OR WITH THE BLACK VIEWER

1 Primary color. Yellow. The four-color model (see color model 2 on page 9) begins at the top, with yellow, one of the four NCS primaries. The color below is the adjacent secondary color, while all those in the column to the right are intermediate, or tertiary, colors.

2 Tertiary color. Yellow-orange. This column of colors shows the intermediate tertiaries between those colors to the left. Complementaries to this column are in the column two spaces to the right, so color 2 is complementary to color 10 and so on.

3 Secondary color. Orange. A NCS secondary. A defect of the NCS four-primary model is the way that perimeter hues are condensed in the blue through to yellow half. Orange hues are a little compromised.

4 Tertiary color. Orange-red. This is a rather condensed area of the NCS palette where blood orange has to sit with scarlet.

5 Primary color. Red. Pure reds are difficult to identify subjectively. This is a NCS primary color.

6 Tertiary color. Red-violet. Magenta occupies this area of the palette, which, like yellow and turquoise, appears tonally lighter and brighter than many other colors, including the primaries, red, green, and blue.

7 Secondary color. Violet. A NCS secondary. Note that the NCS complementary of this is lime green, two spaces to the right of this swatch.

8 Tertiary color. Violet-blue. This is the familiar territory of purple and of ultramarine blue, the exotic color that sits just to the warm side of pure cobalt blue.

This is a technical palette: all the colors here represent principal hues from around the modern four-color wheel that was first theorized by Hering in 1878 and is now the basis of the model of the Natural Color System (NCS). It's a system that has been adopted as several national standards and is particularly used by color professionals and paint and coatings manufacturers worldwide (see color model 2 on page 9).

But that's not the reason this palette is here. It's here because the colors are so in-your-face. Here are sixteen hues of vivid brilliance, as saturated as ink on paper can permit. There is no subtlety here, no ambiguity. Consequently, they all work with each other equally well and equally badly. It's only recently that technical developments in lithographic printing have made the reproduction of these colors possible in normal print. Modern lightfast pigments also now offer these colors for all kinds of industries, so our lives are finally being surrounded by color of an intensity only dreamed of by our forebears of only fifty years ago.

The NCS system, and particularly the combination of the four secondary colors, has had a fundamental influence over fabric, product, and furnishing design in the last five years. Lime green, turquoise, purple, and orange have recently been dominant contemporary colors.

9 Primary color. Blue. An approximation of cobalt blue, i.e. as pure a spectrum blue as possible that moves neither to green nor to red.

10 Tertiary color. Blue-turquoise (cyan). A cool blue equivalent to Prussian blue or phthalo blue.

11 Secondary color. Cyan (turquoise blue). The mid-point between green and blue on the NCS model and an important "new" secondary color.

12 Tertiary color. Cyan-green. A "new" tertiary color that results from the expansion of the blue-green side of the four-color palette, thanks to the introduction of green as a fourth primary. Note that the great majority of seventeenth- and eighteenth-century historical greens were blue-biased (see palette 17).

13 Primary color. Green. The fourth color primary, introduced by Hering. Note the emerald hue of this color.

14 Tertiary color. Yellowish green. It is interesting that many historic colors, especially eighteenth- and nineteenth-century colors, are muted tertiary colors such as this one. Most of the tertiary colors on these pages (i.e. colors 2, 4, 6, 8, 10, 12, 14, and 16) have an equivalent muddy or dusty "period" equivalent. This is less true for primaries and secondaries, mainly due to the imperfection of traditional pigments.

15 Secondary color. Lime green. Lime, turquoise, orange, and purple make up the NCS secondary colors that have been used together so much in the last few years. They constitute a palette of their own.

16 Tertiary color. Lime yellow. This color brings us full circle back to yellow.

VIEW THIS PALETTE AGAINST WHITE

LEFT: The London home of fashion designer Matthew Williamson, clearly a color junky. The bedspread (from Designers Guild) was re-dyed for Matthew and he's even painted the ceiling.

RIGHT: This English house designed by Richard Rogers is dotted with bright secondary and tertiary colors like jewels in a minimalist box.

Of all the cultures that celebrate and revere color, perhaps none is as sophisticated as those of the Andes. There are very few palettes based on historical textiles in this book, partly because the fugitive nature of dyes means they can be historically inaccurate documents of a society's view about color. But the colored fabrics of the Andean Amarus Indians are dyed in an unbroken tradition of techniques and colors that is centuries old, mainly because they believe that the rainbow and its colors have healing and regenerative powers (for example, magenta and fuchsia are connected to courage and innovation). So their society regenerates itself through the recreation of color.

These colors demonstrate just how possible it is to work with intense color—in unusual hues—and still create sophisticated combinations.

1 and 2 This is a palette of complementary relationships that are modified by reducing the intensity of some of the colors with white, and by the inclusion of one pivotal, controlling color— which is not the green. The complementary of green is, well, magenta in one system (additive) and red in others (optical channels and the four-color system). Either way both are present here, together with several variants: the pinks and orange. Use these greens with the more intense complementaries or with the pinks.

3, 4, 5, and 6 This group of reds and pinks is a sophisticated set of near colors with variable amounts of blue, red, and white in them. There is a marked struggle for assertion between them, but this internecine battle is merely a squabble when the group is seen against the greens, blues, or oranges. The overall success of this palette depends on this layered structure of relationships; so the best use of this palette will always involve all the colors.

7 and 8 Even the relationship between these two colors is sharp: one is dark and reddish, the other light and moving toward yellow. The first could be seen as red, but also as orange, just in the way that color 4 could be seen as red or as pink. This occasional ambiguity is a necessary component in the success of this palette. Use these colors with the greens or the pinks. Obscure these other colors to see a rather successful combination of the red-oranges with the blues.

9 and 10 Like the greens, the rich blue has a complementary effect on both the pinks and, particularly, the oranges. The resulting optical effects are shimmering. However, it is the quietest color in the palette, the soft bluish gray-purple color, which is the pivotal element here. In many Andean fabrics it is colors such as this that predominate and form a background against which the brighter hues are displayed. At the very least, a combination of any of these colors can be made to operate together provided this color is included.

OPPOSITE: The lesson of this palette is a simple one repeated throughout the book: purple is as important a color as brown in anchoring a scheme. Never underestimate its importance.

VIEW THIS PALETTE WITH THE GRAY VIEWER

Agnés Emery chose these suitably resort colors for her client's house in Brussels. This is a very demanding palette that requires a lot of manipulation to get right—as she has.

These are seaside colors. You'll find them around the world painted onto the walls of houses, shacks, and cabanas in coastal towns. Portofino in Italy has some of these colors; the English south coast resorts of Weymouth and Dartmouth (for example) have some too. Any seaside resort, especially those that face south, enjoys the luxury of reflected light and, as a result, an increase in overall ambient light levels—in which high levels of contrast and variance of hues can be accommodated.

These vivid colors are, however, historically very important. They are the colors of applied paint, not on buildings but on Roman pottery from Canosa (Canusium), a seaside resort near Bari in Italy: on figurines, busts, and vessels. They demonstrate the brilliance of the pigments available to the classical artist and decorator and are a reminder of how intensely colored the buildings and sculptures of the ancient world probably were.

1 and 7 Two clean blues that are derived from a very mid-blue hue. Consequently, there is very little bias toward either green or purple, which means these colors are straight and uncomplicated. Ideal in a bright, well-lit environment—and with sufficient difference in character to make an interesting combination. Try them with just the pinks or just the flesh tones in this palette.

2, 5, and 8 The most intense pink here is more than a match for the dark blue and can be used in isolation in a scheme with all the blues together. But these pink colors also work well together as a group of three: note how, as for the browns, the paler, more flesh-colored swatch adds interest and stability to the group. For a fresh and harmless combination of seaside colors, look at just the two pale pink swatches with the pale blue swatch.

3, 6, and 9 This family of browns is warm and biased to orange and red. The deep reddish brown is the unmistakable color of iron oxide pigments and the deep orange is that of fine orange-biased cinnabar or even red lead pigment. These three swatches are a palette on their own, in which the palest color underscores all the others.

4 An intense and unbelievably bright yellow from the ancient world, sharp and full in Mediterranean sunlight but one that turns acid under a cloudy sky.

VIEW THIS PALETTE AGAINST WHITE

notes to the palettes

Below is a list of provenances for many of the colors in this book. The numbers refer first to the palette and then to the individual colors within that palette.

All historical wall references are specified as matt and are therefore printed on uncoated paper. Many of the references for painted walls are to extant, conserved examples in museums or in situ. There are obvious problems associated with identifying the colors used by artists hundreds of years ago: principally to do with the way that certain pigments age or discolor in reaction to chemicals present in walls or the atmosphere. All painted surfaces will become dirty in time, but in an attempt to reduce inaccuracy, the following safeguards have been met in color matching references:

1 In order to avoid the misrepresentation of colors that have altered through the effects of age, all source references for wall painting and decoration in the ancient world are extant examples of *buon fresco, fresco secco,* or encaustic painting, processes where the pigments employed are relatively stable and resistant to the effects of alkali, atmospherically borne chemicals, such as sulphur, and ultraviolet radiation. The technique of *buon fresco* (used for example at Pompeii) also requires no medium other than the lime of the wall on which it is applied. The technique of *fresco secco* (used for example in Egyptian wall painting) requires a medium such as gum, casein, or lime, which themselves discolor minimally or not at all. The encaustic technique (used by the Romans, again at Pompeii) involves the suspension of pigment in a purified wax medium that discolors minimally over time and which has been demonstrated to protect the pigment from abrasion and atmospheric pollution much more effectively than either fresco technique.

2 Wherever possible, medieval painted references are derived from furniture and panels painted in egg tempera, a technique wherein the vibrancy of pigments are not in the main altered in the egg medium over time.

3 Furniture, objects, and walls painted in oil colors have not, in the main, been referred to, due to the fact that some oil media darken and deteriorate over time, and some pigments react and discolor in reaction to some oil media over time.

Wall colors from the seventeenth century onward have been matched not to commercial "historic" paint ranges, but to references, samples, and studies of several renowned architectural paint historians (see page 192), directly by comparison with Hexachrome® color swatches and indirectly with a spectrophotometer and translation from Lab or RGB color spaces to Hexachrome®.

Wherever possible, historical paint matches for ancient world wall painting, medieval tempera panel painting, and painted objects have been conducted by comparison of Hexachrome® color swatches with the actual painted object. Further color matching has been possible using a portable spectrophotometer.

The colors of enamels, ceramics, and textiles have been matched by the comparison of Hexachrome® color swatches with the actual object. These colors may have been specified on either coated or uncoated paper depending on the reflectivity of the original source.

Use has been made of source texts (Pliny, Vitruvius, Cennini, Theophrastus) and archaeological and conservation publications in identifying many of the pigments and colors of the ancient and medieval worlds. Descriptions and recipes have been cross-referred to extant examples of painting and decoration from the period.

Wherever possible, historic paint colors on a particular wall or object have also been cross-matched against pigment/media samples. These samples were prepared with reference to historic texts using the appropriate historical medium for the palette source (gum, lime, egg tempera) and painted as massed tone swatches tints or washes as appropriate. In nearly every case, the pigment used was derived from the same source or via the same process as the pigment on the original wall or object (where it was identified). Two examples neatly illustrate this pursuit of authenticity: ultramarine blue pigment was derived from ground lapis lazuli from mines adjacent to the Oxus river in Afghanistan and processed in an identical way to that described by Cennini; "Refiners' Verditer" was also procured according to the eighteenth-century method (as a by-product of silver refining). Here, I am indebted to the artists' colorman Ole Cornelissen and especially to the colorman and hound of pigment authenticity Keith Edwards for their forensic passion. Additionally, historical pigments have been matched, wherever possible, to examples of the minerals from which they would have been ground, deriving from a region known to have supplied that pigment. Examples are limonite, hematite, malachite, azurite, orpiment, and cinnabar.

Palettes 1–16

I have not quite followed the progression of colors in the NCS four-color color wheel (see palette 62), so there are no turquoise/green, green/lime-green, or lime-green/yellow palettes. This is partly a reflection of taste and interest in those parts of the spectrum, but mainly because I have followed the color balance of the Hexachrome® system used to print this book, whereby precise nuances between shades in the green-yellow part of the spectrum can sometimes be lost on the printed page.

If anything, this section follows the traditional system of the subtractive primaries: there are three palettes dedicated to red, yellow, and blue and a further three to the secondary subtractive colors orange, purple, and green. There are a further six tertiary palettes: yellow/orange, etc. There is one change to this structure. I have inserted two tertiary palettes between green and blue: turquoise and cyan, partly as a gesture toward the expansion of the color spectrum in this part of the NCS wheel and partly because of the perceived variance of shades/tints in this part of the six-color process spectrum.

Palette 1

No notes.

Palette 2

1 The term ochre applies to yellow iron oxide earth colors and is a term really reserved for color washed out of sand.

2 Indian yellow is mercifully no longer made, since it was extracted from the urine of cows fed on mango leaves, a diet which did the cows no good.

3 The color of cadmium yellow (since the 1850s and Ridgway "Cadmium Yellow") and of saffron yellow (made from the stigma of crocus sativus; British Colour Council (BCC) "Saffron Yellow"). The latter sounds much more romantic.

7 The color of the pigment Barium yellow.

Palette 3

1 A popular color in the early twentieth century.

2 The right orange for climates with a lot of cloud: its luminance stops it looking too brown. Equivalent to a tint of Ridgway "Cadmium Orange".

3 Produced here by printing Hexachrome® orange ink at 100 percent intensity with nothing else added. Ridgway "Cadmium Orange", and the color of orpiment orange/realgar, native arsenic trisulfide.

4 BCC "Spectrum Orange".

12 Very 1920s and 1970s. Popular as an institutional color.

Palette 4

3 Vermilion is also known as mercuric sulfide. Made according to a method perfected in Holland. Consequently known as "Dutch Vermilion", or since the fourteenth century as "Fire Red". Also called "Poppy Red" in the paint trade and allocated the names "Scarlet" (Ridgway) and "Rouge Grenadier" (Repertoire).

Palette 5

1 This is a near match for the color card named "Vermilion" in the British Royal Horticultural Society's Colour Charts of 1939 and 1941.

2 The color of woollen cloth dyed to a pure red with madder root, a color known in the nineteenth century as "Turkey Red" or "Adrianople Red" and labeled by the RHS as "Orient Red". Another vermilion color and British Post Office red.

3 Oriental laquer was colored with vermilion.

7 Similar to the color chosen by Nicolette Pot of OMA architects, which she calls "NAP".

9 The palest color of Famille Rose porcelain, which was then popularized by Mme de Pompadour in France during the late 1750s.

11 Like color 9, this was first adopted to imitate Oriental ceramics in the seventeenth century, becoming later popular as a decorating color during the first and second French Empires.

12 A Famille Rose color and a tint of the supposed "Rose Pompadour" introduced by Mme de Pompadour.

Palette 6

1 The word "Carmine" comes from the Greek *kermes* and the insect from which reddish dyes could be produced.

2 "Tyrian Purple" is a name that dates from the 1600s.

3 This color is unforgiving and uncompromising because, like the other optical secondary colors, yellow and turquoise, it excites two sets of receptor cone cells in the retina, in this case those for red and blue, communicating literally double the color to the brain as produced when only one set are stimulated.

Palette 7

1 This color has also been known as "Imperial Purple" and amethyst.

Palette 8

1 A tint of one of the first aniline dyes, methyl violet.

2 A color full of historical resonance. The color of ultramarine blue pigment—both the modern synthetic version and its valuable medieval antecedent made from lapis lazuli. Also the color typical of Moorish cobalt-glazed ceramics.

5 These qualities result partly from simple color association (we think of sky as being blue) and partly from an optical phenomenon that creates the impression that blue (and particularly pale or bright blue) appears to recede (whereas reds appear to advance).

9 An illustration of how a tint of an interesting color does not automatically produce an equally useable decorating color.

Palette 9

1 The color chosen by Norman Foster for the HQ of EDF, the French national power company, in Bordeaux.

2 Corresponds to Ridgway "Spectrum Blue" and modern glass frit Egyptian blue pigment bound with gum.

3 Late nineteenth/early twentieth century in feel (together with color 4 to its right).

4 Purple often occurs in this book as a pivotal color in a palette, especially when muted with either gray or brown—or both. When shaded or toned in this way, purple can take on a brooding, bruised look but also an interesting, complex quality. This color and color 12 illustrate just how pleasingly ambiguous purple can be.

5 Similar in character to some of the blue synthetic ultramarine pigments developed by the artist Yves Klein.

7 The color of the bright blue glaze of Persian pottery.

11 This color and color 6 above it are versions of "Korsmo Blue", a color much favored by the eponymous Scandinavian architect for the outside of his buildings. Also a tint of Cerulein blue, a pigment invented in 1859.

14 This is a favorite color of the architect Alessandro Mendini, "Azzurro Nontiscordardime" (forget-me-not blue).

Palette 10

1 The sequence of palettes steps a little out of line on this page, because there are two, not one, palettes between blue and green: this one, and cyan and turquoise over the page.

14 The color often historically used for aircraft undersides and similar to the British Colour Council's "Sky Grey" of 1934.

Palette 11

1 The kind of blue that appears on Middle and Far Eastern ceramics. An optical secondary color and thus bright to look at.

2 Another ceramic and very marine color.

3 The color of deep viridian pigment and a tint of modern phthalocyanine green.

5 Similar to coal-tar dye color "Capri Blue" produced by Bender in 1890.

7 An intense Georgian and 1920s Georgian revival shade, a tint of chrysocolla pigment (a naturally occurring copper compound used by the ancients).

Palette 12

1 It's the color of nickel arsenate (the mineral cabrerite) and is known as "Nickel Green".

4 This color appears on exterior woodwork and gates in modern Paris.

5 A relatively intense tint of malachite or "Mountain Green", an ancient pigment.

10 Also used in the eighteenth century and known as "Mineral Green" (see palette 17 for more common colors of the eighteenth century).

13 A tint of malachite.

16 This is Sung green, the color of porcelain from the eponymous Chinese period.

Palette 13

7 It's also the color of uranium salts and is known as "Uranium Green".

9 This standard method of dying green persisted until the late nineteenth century.

14 Also a tint of the green much used by the painter Veronese.

16 Grays are difficult to get right, since black produces hard, bluish tints. Umber grays are flexible but greenish grays are fresher.

Palette 14

No notes.

Palette 15

1 A good color for leather, ceramic cookware, and 1970s car interiors. Not so good for painting the bedroom ceiling.

2 A color that historically was often used indoors and out (in Roman wall painting, for example). Consequently a classical revival color.

3 Traditionally a useful pigment for glazing (oil painting, wood graining, etc.) because of its transparency.

6 A mid-toned iron oxide that is like brown shoe polish. Another color much used in history.

8 Almost beige or manila, more like a tint of raw umber, since it has a slight greenish cast.

9 This color is redolent of varnished pine. Use it if you ever want to see that color again.

10 The most prized brown pigments in history were those with a clean orange bias. This is similar in color to the best of them, an earth from Pozzuoli in Italy.

Palette 16

No notes.

Palette 17

This palette is derived entirely from Patrick Baty's work in the field of historical color research. A full palette of 64 colors has been published, and hand-painted swatch cards and paint in a variety of media in these colors can be bought from Papers and Paints Ltd, 4 Park Walk, London SW10 0AD, United Kingdom, www.colourman.com. Some colors, notably some of the "common colors" such as "Lead Color", "Dark Stone", and "Cream Color" have not been reproduced here because of the technical limitations of printing this volume: in particular, dark bluish green-grays do not reproduce well.

Patrick Baty's published range has been selected from three sources: some are color matches to early paint recipes; some depend on his own study and analysis of paint colors from historic buildings, together with the research work of Dr Ian Bristow; some are color matches to painters' cards from 1807. The range is a selective representation of some of the more popular colors of the period that are mentioned in contemporary texts.

Additionally, colors cross-match to samples of pigment known to be available in the period, notably the earth colors and green and blue verditer, which conform in hue to pigment being produced by the colorman Keith Edwards, according to historical recipes.

Further references are given in the text to some similar colors that have been found on buildings in America. These are published in the 1994 volume *Paint in America* and represent the research of the color analyst Frank S. Welsh, who has done much to dispel fictional ideas about America's historical colors. He has published a list of 35 colors from various important historic sites in America, which are strikingly similar to many colors in this palette. His published list contains Lab measurements for each color, which have been referred to in cross-matching his references to Baty's paints with a spectrometer (set at illuminant C, 2 degree angle). Only the Welsh colors that most closely approximate Baty's colors have been referred to. Full paint samples of the American colors can be bought from Frank S. Welsh at PO Box 767, Bryn Mawr, PA 19010, USA. See the bibliography for fuller details of the volume mentioned, together with other research work.

Palette 18

British Standard Colours for Ready-Mixed Paints, No. 381C (this reference still applies to a British color range, chiefly paints for technical use, and most of the original colors, the battleship grays excepting, are still included in it), taken from a 1931 color card issued by the British Engineering Standards Association (BESA). Also *BESA Proposed Standard Shades*, plate XV in A. Seymour Jennings' *Paint and Colour Mixing*, seventh edition, 1926.

BESA colors were being experimented with earlier in the century, but were only standardized by a large committee of interested parties in 1925–26 that was appointed by the BESA to deal not only with colors but coating materials and raw ingredients. One sub-panel was appointed to allocate names to paint colors and, having collected all the available manufacturers' shade cards, found that under accepted common terms, such as "Sky Blue" a wide range of colors was available on the market. This is a problem they rectified with the first 381C range and the standard names given in this palette are those chosen by that panel.

Other national standards had been introduced in the first two decades of the century, but none had been created for the paint trade. Robert Ridgway, a Bird Curator in Washington, USA, had published *Color Standards and Color Nomenclature*, a reference system of 53 plates of colored swatches based on the color wheel, intended for natural history color identification. Also in the USA, the Textile Color

Card Association of the United States of America had published the *Standard Color Card of America*, a swatch card of 106 colored silk ribbons for identifying dye colors. In France, M.H. Dauthenay had edited the *Repertoire des Couleurs, par la Société Française des Chrysanthesmistes*, a collection of 365 plates in two portfolios of color tints and shades to be used for identifying the colors of fruit, flowers, and foliage. All proved useful contributions to understanding color and codifying it. All were used in disciplines well beyond the spheres for which they were created. All acknowledged the difficulty of how to name colors.

Palette 19

1–12 From the "Alabastine" range of water-based interior wall paints from the Alabastine Company (British) Ltd. From the full color card published in A. Seymour Jennings' *Paint and Colour Mixing*, seventh edition, 1926.

13–22 From the "Nayrodec" range of water-based interior wall paints from Naylor Brothers (London) Ltd. From Jennings *op. cit.*

Palette 20

1–6 From a proposed color scheme for a dining room; the main color in this proposal was the gray-brown and the secondary color lime green.

7–10 From a proposed color scheme for a library; the main color in this proposal was the violet-gray and the secondary color dark battleship gray. Note that two minor colors in the original proposal, a deep empire green and a blue-gray have been omitted from this book. All from Elizabeth Burris-Meyer's *Contemporary Color Guide*, New York, 1947.

Palette 21

1–5 From a design for a proposed apartment living room by Raymond Rust, mid-1950s; V&A Museum, London.

Palette 22

1–4 From a wallpaper designed by Lucienne Day, "Limited Editions 1951" series, manufactured by John Line & Sons Ltd., 1951; V&A Museum, London.

5–8 From "Triad" furnishing fabric designed by Lucienne Day, screen-printed rayon satin, Heals Wholesale and Export Ltd., 1955; V&A Museum, London.

Palette 23

1–5 From a textile design by Eddie Squires; V&A Museum, London.

Palette 24

1–5 From a wallpaper designed by Eddie Squires, "Colortron", Warner and Sons Ltd., 1967; V&A Museum, London.

Palette 25

1 From a Fiorenza chair, designed by Motomi Kawakami, manufactured by Alberto Bazzani, ABS plastic; V&A Museum, London.

2 From a Pastilli Chair, designed by Eero Aarnio, fibreglass and polyester resin, 1968; Asko, Lahti, Finland.

3 From a chair designed by Joe Colombo, plywood with polyester varnish, 1963; Kartell, Milan, Italy.

4 From a stacking chair designed by Verner Panton, fibreglass and polyester resin, 1960; Herman Miller Furniture Co., Michigan, USA.

5 From an armchair designed by Ernest Race, 1946; Ernest Race Ltd, London, UK.

6 From a "Toga" stacking chair, designed by Sergio Mazza, hot press mould fibreglass, 1968; Artemide, Italy.

7 From a chair designed by Pierre Paulin, 1966; Artifort, Netherlands.

8 From a "Oberon" garden seat, designed by H.W. Wood MBE, 1964; Lurashell.

Palette 26

1–4 *The Book of Historical Colours*, Thos. Parsons & Sons Ltd, 1937 (reprint). By kind permission of Patrick Baty.

Palette 27

1 From interior wall color, ballroom, Lidingsberg, Sweden.

4 and 7 From interior woodwork and walls, manor, Olivehult, Sweden.

5–8 From painted dados, woodwork, and furniture, traditional farmsteads, Skåne, Denmark.

Palette 28

All the swatches in palettes 28 and 29 were matched against camouflage scheme colors of various air forces and navies. However, as with all the palettes in this book, no guarantee can be given that colors have been reproduced utterly faithfully. Nor is this palette in any way comprehensive. With thanks to Humbrol paints.

1, 4, 7, and 10 Russian Air Force.

2 "Duck Egg Blue"; RAF, European.

3 Blue FS35414; USAF Navy and Marine, contemporary.

5 "Gris Bleu Clair" (light blue-gray); French Air Force.

6 "Hellblau" (light blue); Luftwaffe, World War II.

8 Light gray; generic naval vessels.

9 "Himmelblau" (sky blue); Luftwaffe, World War II.

11 "PRU Blue"; RAF post-war.

12 "Azure Blue"; RAF overseas.

Palette 29

1–4 All from USAF, Vietnam.

1 Upper-surface green olive drab.

2 Upper-surface dark green. Also base color, disruptive pattern, UK forces, Burma 1942.

3 Under-surface gray.

4 Upper-surface tan.

5 Matt pale stone; base color, British military two-color disruptive pattern, North Africa 1937,1939, 1940, 1942, Syria, Persia, and Iraq 1943.

6 German overall sand; tanks, World War II.

7 Afrika Korps desert yellow; military vehicles, World War II.

8 Eighth Army desert yellow.

9 "Pink Panther" pink; modified lightweight Land Rover color as used by SAS commandos in the 1991 Gulf War. Matched to a vehicle currently at Blandford Forum.

10 British military two-color disruptive pattern, North Africa 1939 and 1942, Syria, Persia, and Iraq 1943.

11 Base color; British military three-color disruptive pattern, Europe 1939 and North Africa 1943.

12 Japanese airforce mauve.

Palette 30

1–7 Construction sites.

8 "Red Oxide of Iron Paint" (formulated with linseed oil and very pure iron oxide pigment) manufactured to paint the Forth Rail Bridge. Courtesy of Craig and Rose paint manufacturers, Edinburgh.

Palette 31

1 This is usually a refined clay containing silica, colored by the presence of iron oxides and can be extracted from ochreous sand, clay deposit,s and goethite (a form of limonite $FeO(OH).nH_2O$).

2 Because of their muddy complexity, yellows and creams made with ochre and white tend not to turn greenish under natural daylight from an overcast or North sky. As a result, ochre is an invaluable color for decoration and is now chemically synthesized for mass production of paints and coatings.

3 Naturally occurring mineral pigments vary in color and intensity around the world according to their purity. An ochre with high levels of hydrated ferrous oxide will look stronger.

5 If Goethite or yellow ochre are heated, they give off water molecules and turn, irreversibly, red (becoming anhydrous ferric oxide). This is something you can try with yellow ochre pigment and a gas ring. The naturally occurring equivalent red mineral is hematite (Fe_2O_3), which is found in several colors, the most common of which is cool and slightly purplish. Spanish red is the name for the impure pigment and Indian red that for the purer, more intense versions.

6 If the intense purplish hue of some hematite reds is too strong and uncompromising for many uses, then the tints it produces with white are equally accessible, useable, and pretty.

9 The deepest hematites have a brownish shade due to the presence of manganese oxides in the pigment. This is a similar color to a warm red ochre but deeper. In fact the finest shades are the most intense of all the earth colors and are made by calcining (roasting) raw sienna pigment to drive off water molecules and produce a deep red pigment with intense fiery undertones that become visible when the color is diluted.

10 This pigment is again a clay colored with iron oxides and manganese, and is mined as the mineral glauconite.

13 Although the classification of earth pigments breaks down into yellows and reds with the addition of manganese in some cases, in practice there are six basic terms of which yellow ochre and red ochre are the brightest pair and raw sienna and burnt sienna are their slightly duller equivalents. They take their name from the Italian city of Siena, from around which the finest grades of raw sienna could once be found.

15 The color is a feature of the particle size of hematite (which is black before being pulverized): 0.5 microns produces violet-red, while 0.1 microns produces red.

17 The more manganese there is in an earth pigment, the blacker it will appear.

19 Hematite will also produce an orange pigment if the particles are ground even finer (to 0.05 microns).

21 The manganese in raw umber turns the brilliance of the iron oxide present in yellow ochre into a deep greenish brown.

22 When black is mixed with white the resulting grays are almost always blue-tinged and slightly unnatural.

23 When raw umber is calcined (roasted) it loses its yellowish greenness and becomes the deepest brown of all the earth colors. It also becomes more transparent.

Palette 32

1–8 From faded Verdure tapestry colors from several sources. See also Thos. Parsons & Sons Ltd, *Historical Colours*, London, 1937 (and earlier editions), for alternative conjectural tapestry colors.

Palette 33

From a variety of paint manufacturers' shade cards.

1 Also appears on much Shaker painted furniture, especially chairs and stands.

4 Matches several early Pennsylvanian Dutch pieces in the collection of the American Museum, Bath.

5 From a counter painted dark blue at The Shaker Museum, Old Chatham, New York, c.1815.

7 From a painted chest painted in blue-green by Z. Winchester at the Hancock Shaker Village, Pittsfield, Massachusetts. Dated 1821.

Palette 34

1–6 All from pottery: amphorae, cups, and other vases from Athens and Rhodes, 600–400 BC; British Museum, London.

Palette 35

1–6 From Turkish tiles and Mosque lamps, some from the Piyale Pasha Mosque, Istanbul, and the Yeni Valide Cami Mosque, Iznik, 1550–70.

7 From a Syrian panel from Damascus, supposedly from the Sinaniye Mosque; V&A Museum, London. All the colors are present in the numerous architectural tile schemes of Samarkand, notably on the mosque of Bibi Khanom (1398), the dome of the Gur-e Amir (1398), and the madrasah of Shir Doh (1619).

Palette 36

1–8 All from Roman stone tesserae mosaics from Halicarnassus and Ephesus in Turkey, Carthage, and Utica in Tunisia. British Museum, London.

Palette 37

1–12 All from Roman stone tesserae mosaics from Halicarnassus and Ephesus in Turkey, Carthage, and Utica in Tunisia. British Museum, London.

Palette 38

1 From a bowl, single color, Song dynasty, 960–1279; V&A Museum, London.

2 Export color, from various ceramic items, seventeenth century onward.

3 From a bowl, single color, Song dynasty, 960–1279; V&A Museum, London.

4 From a teapot, single color, Dehua ware, Ming-Qing dynasty, 1620–1700; V&A Museum, London.

5 From a bowl, single color, Song dynasty, 960–1279; V&A Museum, London.

6 From a jar, single color, Yuan dynasty, 1350–1400; V&A Museum, London.

Palette 39

1–4 Listed in *The Colours of Japan* by Sadao Hibi (see introductory essay by Kunio Fukuda for a description of traditional terms). Mayer (1981) gives a list of Japanese pigments, principal among which are vermilion (cinnabar red), azurite (blue), malachite (greenish blue), and a variety of whites with different surface qualities, ground from shells, mica, quartz, or calcite.

1 Matched to a sample of Chinese cinnabar (mercuric sulfide) from Yuanshanchiang; Natural History Museum, London. This pigment is recognized as one of the oldest in widespread use in Japanese culture.

4 Matches a sample of azurite pigment from Thuringia; Natural History Museum, London. Japan still imports azurite from America (Mayer, 1981) and samples from Morenci and the Copper Queen mine in Arizona (held in the NHM London) show a deep blue capable of producing a pigment of this intensity.

Note that some sources consider the original meaning of the four color terms to represent light and dark, clear and vague, a construct similar in form to Aristotle's color scale on which all colors (but principally red and green) stood in relation to darkness and light. His model persisted in Western culture until the Renaissance and, it would appear, therefore ran parallel with the suggested Japanese meanings.

Palette 40

1 From a red silk hat, Qing dynasty, nineteenth century; V&A Museum, London.

2 From various lacquer objects, from the seventeenth to twentieth centuries, and matched to modern sourced manufactured Chinese vermilion.

3 From a porcelain vase, Kangxi period, Qing Dynasty, 1662–1722, China; V&A Museum, London.

4 From eighteenth-century Chinese robes, also Repertoire "Jaune Indien" 27/2 and RHS "Chinese Yellow" 60/6.

Palette 41

1–3 All taken from designs executed in watercolor for lead-glazed creamware; The English Archive. Also from ceramic "zellij" tilework, columns, Sahriz Mandrasah, Fez (1321–26).

Palette 42

Percentage figures in printing denote the dot density for each color and therefore what amount of each color is being used. It does not denote the percentage quantity of each ink as part of the finished color. Thus it is possible to have, say, a dark brown comprising 100 percent magenta, 100 percent yellow and 40 percent black.

1–3 From 1960s and 1970s magazines, including *Vogue*, *House & Garden*, and *Connaissance*, in the collection of the author. Also see Lesley Jackson's *Contemporary*, London, 1994, which illustrates many period objects and interiors with original photography and printed imagery, especially pages 106, 109, 118–19, and 132.

Also these colors appear together in Middle Egyptian wall paintings: see Gustave Jequier's *Décoration Egyptienne*, Paris, 1911, Pls XXVI and XXVIII; painted ceiling in the tomb of Hepuseneb, Thebes, 1495–75 BC and Tombs of Amemheb and Nebamon at Thebes, 1400s BC.

Palette 43

1–2 Matched to a variety of vehicles in the Beaulieu Motor Museum and the Haynes Collection, UK.

3 This color is matched to the Gordon Bennett Napier of 1903 at the National Motor Museum, UK. It is a British Standard (BS381C) color, "Deep Brunswick Green", the color that Bentleys raced in at Le Mans during the 1920s and which outsold all other colors on British MG sports cars throughout the twentieth century by a factor of four to one.

The origin of the color is apocryphal, but the first allocation of colors to different countries' racing teams came about for the first world international series of motor races organized by James Gordon Bennett in 1899. The rules, laid out by the Automobile Club de France, allocated red to the Americans, blue to the French, yellow for Belgium, and white for Germany. In fact, very few teams stuck to these requirements for the first few years, and the association of Britain with green occurred through happenstance. In 1901 the British driver Charles Jarrott made a visit to the French workshops that were preparing his 40hp Panhard for that year's Paris–Berlin race. The workshop owner had ordered the car to be painted a "beautiful, rich dark" green because the car had been allocated the number 13 for the race, and green being a lucky color in France, he thought the new color would ward off the ill effects of the number. A year later Britain won the Gordon Bennett race with SF Edge, it is reported, driving a green Napier (the previous year it had been a red Napier). This meant that in 1903 the British had to host the event but could not, due to parliamentary restrictions concerning road races. Ireland proved to be a compromise location and apparently, to honor their hosts, the British team painted all their cars green—the Irish national color.

In 1905 national racing colors were reintroduced and black allocated to the Italians. They quickly objected, insisting on green, a stripe of their tricolor. Since by this time the Americans had lost interest in European races, a compromise appears to have been reached and by the following year, all Italian sports cars were being painted the old American color, red (another color in the Italian national flag). More arguments followed, more countries joined the races, and more teams defied the regulations until after World War I when, finally, national teams got on with the business of competitive driving rather than competitive grooming. The final positions were: red for Italy, blue for France, white (and later silver) for Germany, green for Britain. The national prejudices survive today. Ferraris are still red, Porsches, Audis and Mercedes still silver, and what's left of British car manufacturing occasionally dips its brush in a pot of green paint. Extracted from archive material at the National Motor Museum, in particular publicity for the Coys International Historic Festival, notes of the BRDC, and the April 1990 edition of *British Racing Green* with an article by Bill Boddy.

Palette 44

1–6 Cotton fragment made in Burhampur, eighteenth-century; Murghal floorspread, cotton and silk, Gujarati, late seventeenth- or early eighteenth-century; Murghal loose tent hangings, late seventeenth century. All V&A Museum, London.

Note these colors also appear in Qanat panels of the period.

Palette 45

1–3 From a Forziere (marriagechest) painted with foliage; Tuscan, 1350; V&A Museum, London.

3–4 From a chest painted with foliage; Romanian, nineteenth century; collection of the author.

4 From a Cassone (large box) with a depiction of Susannah and the Elders by Francesco di Giorgio; Pinacoteca Nazionale, Siena.

5–6 From a Cassone panel; Sienese,1475. V&A Museum, London.

Palette 46

1 From a porcelain wine cup, Qing dynasty, Kangxi mark and period (1662–1722); British Museum, London.

2 From a porcelain wine cup, Qing dynasty, Yongzheng mark and period (1723–35).

3–4 From a Sèvres teapot, Bowes Museum, Barnard Castle. A very similar pink appears on a decorated Qing dynasty porcelain teapot (1740–80) in the V&A Museum, London.

5 From 21/1 RHS color charts. Parsons' *Historical Colours*.

6 From Parsons' *Historical Colours* by kind permission of Patrick Baty.

Palette 47

1–4 "Riddarateppid" (Coverlet of Knights), seventeenth century; Thjødminjasafn Islands, Reykjavik. Eight Point Star cushion, seventeenth century; Nordiska Museet, Stockholm.

Palette 48

1–5 From a wall painting panel, Palace of Cnossos, Crete; British Museum, London. Colorwork principally in red and blue with yellow. Linework in near-black. The red is undoubtedly hematite; the yellow of the period was ochre, although here it may have been overglazed (the color is more indicative of orpiment, a naturally occurring arsenic trisulfide). The blue is probaby Egyptian blue, a finely powdered glass frit colored with copper compounds that was known to the Minoans. It could also be a simple tint of azurite (this color corresponds to a tint of a modern sample of calcareous Moroccan azurite, known as "Blue Bice" in the collection of Keith Edwards). The blue-black corresponds to their use of powdered slate as a pigment. Further colors such as green were made possible by intermixing pigments (Mayer, 1981).

This palette also appears in the following locations: textile patterns from the Procession Fresco at Cnossos, about 1550–1400 BC; textile patterns from a fresco at Hagia Triada, about 1700–1600 BC; fresco fragment showing columns from Cnossos, about 1700–1550 BC; fresco ornament from Cnossos, about 1550 BC; also in Greece, floor paintings in the palace at Tiryns, about 1400–1200 BC (H. Bossert's *An Encyclopaedia of Colour Decoration*, Wasmuth, 1928 and H. Bossert's *Alltkreta*, second edition, 1923); also in Etruscan Italy at Tarquinia, fresco in the "Tomba delle Leonesse", first half of the six century BC; frescoes in the "Tomba dei Leopardi" and "Tomba del Triclinio", about 500 BC; fresco in the "Tomba del Tifone", third and second centuries BC (F. Weege, *Etruskische Malerei*, Halle, 1921 and H. Bossert, *An Encyclopaedia of Colour Decoration*, Wasmuth, 1928.

Palette 49

1–5 From wall paintings at Cacaxtla, near Mexico City; early Mayan (although outside Mayan territory), 650–900 AD. The red and yellow have been identified by Diana Magaloni as containing hematite and limonite respectively (*National Geographic*, Vol. 182, No. 3, September 1992). The blues are almost certainly Maya blue, a pigment developed for wall painting and ceramics in pre-conquest Meso-America and made by precipitating indigo onto the white clay mineral, attapulgite (Gettens, 1962, and Kleber *et.al.*, 1967).

Palette 50

No notes.

Palette 51

1–4 Watercolor by Robert Smirke, c. 1802; Drawings Collection, Royal Institute of British Architects, London. Also illustrated in J.C. Krafft and N. Ransonette, *Plans, Coups, Élevations des plus belles Maisons et Hôtels construits à Paris et dans les Environs*, Paris, 1802. See also P. Thornton, *Authentic Décor*, Weidenfeld & Nicolson, London, 1984, pl. 241.

Palette 52

1 From wallpaper border, 1820–30; A.L. Courtan gift, V&A Museum, London.

1 and 3 Also appear together in Nathaniel Whittock's *The Decorative Painters' and Glaziers' Guide* (London, 1827) as a family of rather brilliant colors for simulating a variety of "fancy woods" for "shop fronts, halls, &tc", including rosewood, red satinwood and coralwood.

4 From a silk panel manufactured by Joseph Dory, Lyon, 1813; V&A Museum, London.

5 From wall and fabric colors from a watercolor proposal for a bedchamber design in the Empire style, based on classical models; Théodore Pasquier, *Dessins d'ameublement*, Paris, c. 1830, Bibliothèque Forney, Paris. See also Peter Thornton, *Authentic Décor*, London, 1984, pl. 324.

Palette 53

This palette was assembled from commonly recurrent architectural colors. Notable examples only are given.

1 From walls in buildings, Thar desert, India, and house colors in villages of Olympos, Menetes, Arkassa, and Volada, Karpathos islands, Greece, recorded in *Les couleurs de L'europe* by Jean-Philippe Lenclos, Moniteur, France, 1995.

2 From city walls of Taroudant and Kasbahs in rammed earth, Ksour (fortified villages), Morocco.

3 From Greek islands as color 1 and mud houses, Thar desert, India. Also nomadic huts in coastal Gujarat.

4 From mud houses, Thar desert, India, and walls of Taroudant, Essaouira, and Kasbahs in the Dades valley, South Sahara.

5 From Greek islands as color 1 and houses at Burano, Naples, Italy.

6 From mud walls and houses in the villages of Mzonda, Rissani, and Tinerhir, Morocco.

7 From applied color, houses in the Thar desert, India.

8 As color 6 and also shutters/garages/details of houses in Essaouira and Taroudant plain, Morocco, and applied color to houses in Burano, Naples.

9 From ceiling of Bahia Palace, Marrakesh and walls in the Brahmpari (city of Brahmins), Jodhpur. Also clothes worn by Sahraouis nomads, Sahara desert, the "blue men of the Sahara".

10 From walls at a coastal farmhouse, near Essaouira and walls of Old Palace, Taroudant, Morocco.

11 From wall color at Chaouen (between Tangiers and Fes, Morocco), and Brahmpari, Jodhpur (see above).

12 From woodwork, farmhouses near Essaouira; indigo-dyed clothing of the Sahraouis; doors at Chaouen; a shade of the color of the Merinid dynasty (1269–1465). All Morocco.

13 From Brahmpari, Jodhpur (see above).

14 From nomadic huts in coastal Gujarat.

15 From detail color on buildings in the Thar desert and also near Tadpatri, Andhra Pradesh (with color 16). Detail color at Nimaj Haveli (former townhouse), Jodhpur; all India. Also town walls of El Jorf and at Chaouen, Morocco. Note this tone of turquoise nearly always accompanies color 16, as a detail color.

16 Also the color of Portuguese window frames, Greek villages and the darkest walls in the holy city of Jodhpur. Also, in western culture, the blue of the Madonna's robes, French medieval royalty and washing blue. Similar to the blue of Villa Majorelle, Marrakesh. Also house colors in villages of Karpathos islands, Greece (see above). Also Brahmpari, Jodhpur, India. It is commonly associated with color 15.

Palette 54

1–4 All from Lagoan house, Flores, El Petén, Guatemala; exterior wall colors, Calle Noche Triste, Oxaca, Mexico; exterior wall colors, Rio Lagartos, Yucatan, Mexico.

Palette 55

1–3 Postulated and formulated to historical descriptions given in *Japanese Detail* by Hibi Sadao with an introductory essay by Kunio Fukuda.

1 The green *moegi* was produced by overdyeing yellow plant dyes with indigo (Japan had a thriving domestic trade in indigo-dyed cloth from early times). Fukuda notes that silk dyed in this way generally turned out an attractive yellow, while cotton turned drab olive green.

2 Note that in Japan brown became classified as a color in its own right only in the Edo period and was referred to as *chairo* ("tea color"). By the late eighteenth century, shades of brown were being named after famous Kabuki actors.

Palette 56

1–4 From an illustration by Eric Bagge of a bedroom designed by Louis Süe and André Mare (partners from 1919–28 and the founders of the Compagnie des Arts Français). See L. Moussinac, *Intérieurs*, 1924; Bibliothèque Nationale, Paris. In partnership with the artist Mare, Süe designed interiors for among others, Helena Rubinstein, Jean Patou and the ocean liners *Normandie* and *Ile de France*.

Palette 57

1–3 From a 1972 copy of the Volkswagen Microbus sales catalogue.

4 Matched to a vehicle.

Palette 58

1–4 NCS color palette.

Palette 59

1 Virgin and Child; V&A Museum, London.

2 Virgin and Child; V&A Museum, London.

3 Foliage and clothing color, roundel and shrine panel; V&A Museum, London.

4 Clothing and "shadow" color, frieze; Ospedale del Ceppo, Pistoia.

5 Foliage color, coats of arms, The Annunciation and other panels; Ospedale del Ceppo, Pistoia; large round panel, V&A Museum, London.

6 Various panels, V&A Museum, London.

7 Foliage color, coats of arms, The Annunciation and other panels; Ospedale del Ceppo, Pistoia; large round panel, V&A Museum, London.

8 Various panels, V&A Museum, London.

9 Coat of Arms of the Medici, Ospedale del Ceppo, Pistoia. Various panels, V&A Museum, London.

10 Various panels, V&A Museum, London.

Palette 60

1–2 From a food box, Jaijing reign, 1522–66, China, V&A Museum, London.

3–6 From an alcohol jar, China; V&A Museum, London.

7–8 From a Ming porcelain food box, Jaijing reign, China.

9–10 From a porcelain flask, Yuan dynasty, c. 1350, China, V&A Museum, London.

11–14 From cobalt glazed Arita pottery, 1600 onward, Japan; various tems, V&A Museum, London.

Palette 61

1–4 Until the 1850s, all dyestuffs were natural. Dyers had to rely on plant-based products such as indigo and madder, the separate supply industries for which were vast. Essentially, very little was known about the chemical properties of dyes until the advent of modern organic chemistry, which more or less started at this time. One man in particular, William Henry Perkins, deserves mentioning, since it was while searching for a cure for malaria in 1856 that he accidentally produced an intense synthetic dye, which he called mauve. It was not stable in UV light and faded, so our modern understanding of the name mauve does not convey the excitement this discovery created, nor the influence the color was to have in fashion of the period.

Perkins' color was the first in a range of simple aniline, or coal-tar, dyes. Many others quickly followed, including the first synthetic alizarin dye in 1868, which posed the first serious threat to the traditional plant-based dye trade. Later azo-type and sulphur-based dyes were more permanent and formed the basic building blocks of modern colorant chemistry that has allowed every one of us to enjoy color as a freely available property of the modern world.

1 Mauve; simple aniline (coal-tar) dye, Perkins, 1856. Silk dress dyed with Perkins' original dye, c. 1862, Science Museum, London. Origin of the term mauve is from malva, the latin for mallow, mauve being the French term for the plant.

2 Magenta, simple aniline (coal-tar) dye, Verguin, 1858–9. The second basic dye, and more widely used than mauve. Also known as "Fuchsin". BCC "Magenta" 198.

3 Alizarin crimson, synthetic madder, the first example of a synthesized vegetable dye, Graebe and Liebermann, Germany, 1868, and Perkins, independently in England. Ridgway "Rose Red" 71, modern Alizarin crimson, artists' pigment, RHS "Crimson".

4 Methyl violet, basic dye, Lauth, 1861. Similar to Ridgway "Bluish Violet" 57 and RHS "Methyl Violet".

Palette 62

1–16 NCS color palette.

Palette 63

Admittedly, the Andeans have had generations to get it right, but this palette is masterful. And, like many of the most interesting palettes in history, it relies on purple as a pivotal color.

1–10 From clothes, shawls, and fabrics from the Urubamba valley, Pisac and Cuzco markets, Peru.

Palette 64

Some colors appear on more than one object.

1, 3, 4, and 9 Askos (spouting jar), made in Canosa, Italy, 270–200 BC.

2, 3, 5, and 8 From terra-cotta figures, made in Canosa, Italy, 270–200 BC.

2 and 7 Statuette of a woman with a duck and a conch shell, made in Canosa, Italy, 270–200 BC.

6 Rhyton (drinking horn), red-figured, from Capra.

All decorated in paint over a white slip ground on terra-cotta. From the Steuart and Durand collections, British Museum, London.

No analyses of pigments have been conducted on the artifacts in these collections, but x-ray diffraction, chemical, and UV analyses have been conducted on other polychrome objects of the period, notably by R.A. Higgins in 1970. They identified a wide variety of paint pigments in use, including ochres and hematites, soot or bituminous blacks, chalk, gypsum, malachite, and Egyptian blue.

Color 3 is the color of a pigment from a mine at Pozzuoli in Italy, known to the Romans at this time, producing a strong, warm red ochre, which famously became known as Pozzuoli red. Matched to a modern sample of pigment produced at Pozzuoli and to a sample of the pozzolanic rock from the mine at Pozzuoli, courtesy Keith Edwards.

Color 6 is extremely close to a sample of medieval formula vermilion formerly sold by the pigment company Kremer, and a good tonal match for a sample of cinnabar mined at Mount Amiata in Tuscany. Both in the collection of Keith Edwards.

Color 4 is the color of very pure orpiment, rarely found as free of orange as this. However, it is more likely to be a lead yellow glaze, used in conjunction with polychrome painting on pottery of this period.

The blues in this palette suggest the use of a very pure azurite with little green content. Color 1 matches a modern paint, in both gum and egg tempera, of azurite pigment from the Tsumeb mine in Namibia. However, the use of Egyptian blue pigment (cobalt or copper glass frit) was widespread at this time as a decorative ceramic paint color in Greece (see above). Riederer (*Artists' Pigments*, Vol. 3, 1976) identified it on Greek painted vases at Centuripe in Sicily from the second century BC. Egyptian blue was also known as Pozzuoli blue.

The pinks in this palette could be derived from one of several sources: the same murex shellfish that produced the extremely expensive dyes used for coloring fine cloths of the period; a madder lake (more likely) formed by precipitating an intense dye made from the roots of madder plants onto an inert base such as chalk; or a pigment manufactured from the kermes insect. Color 2 is the color of a modern genuine rose madder lake massed in gum, but this color is also closely related to a pigment sample in Keith Edwards' collection of modern Indian lake (lac), formulated from insects that are similar to the kermes insect. Higgins identified madder as the colorant in one analysis but failed to identify the pink colorant of one thespian statue of 450 BC (1970). However, W.T. Russell (1892) and Farnsworth (1951) separately identified madder lake as the colorant in samples of processed pigments from Egypt and Corinth dating from the Greco-Roman period, making it the most likely source for these colors.

For a full discussion of these pigments see Riederer, Schweppe and Winter in *Artists' Pigments*, Vol. 3, (1997).

bibliography

In addition to the works mentioned in the Notes to the Palettes on pages 176–185, here is a core bibliography.

history of color, pigments, and color in decoration

Philip Ball, *Bright Earth: The Invention of Colour*, Viking, 2001.

Jenny Balfour-Paul, *Indigo*, British Museum Press, London, 1998.

Patrick Baty, "Palette of Historic Paints", *Country Life Magazine*, 20 February 1992, UK.

Patrick Baty, "Palette of the Past", *Country Life Magazine*, 3 September 1992, UK.

Paul Binski, *Medieval Craftsmen: Painters*, British Museum Press, London, 1991.

Viola and Rosamund Borradaile, *Practical Tempera Painting: A Student's Cennini*, Dolphin, Brighton, 1949.

Helmuth Bossert, *An Encyclopaedia of Colour Decoration*, Ernst Wasmuth, Berlin, 1928.

Ian C. Bristow, *Architectural Colour in British Interiors, 1615–1840*, Yale University Press, London, 1996.

Ian C. Bristow, *Interior House-Painting Colours and Technology, 1615–1840*, Yale University Press, London, 1996.

Ian C. Bristow, "Ready-Mixed Paint in the Eighteenth Century", *Architectural Review*, No. 963, April 1977.

Ian C. Bristow, "Repainting Eighteenth-century Interiors", *ASCHB transactions 1981* (vol. vi, 1982).

M. Brusatin, *A History of Colors*, Shambala, Boston, USA, 1991.

E.R. Caley, "Ancient Greek Pigments", *Journal of Chemical Education*, 23 (1946).

Robert Chenciner, *Madder Red*, Curzon Press, 2000.

François Delamare and Bernard Guineau, *Colour, Making and Using Dyes and Pigments*, trans. from the French edition, Thames and Hudson, London, 2000.

Alan Dronsfield and John Edmonds, *The Transition from Natural to Synthetic Dyeing*, Edmonds, 2001.

John Edmonds, *The History of Woad and the Medieval Woad Vat*, Edmonds, 1998.

John Edmonds, *The History and Practice of Eighteenth-century Dyeing*, Edmonds, 1999.

John Edmonds, *Tyrian or Imperial Purple Dye*, Edmonds, 2000.

English Heritage, *Layers of Understanding, Proceedings of Architectural Paint Seminar*, Donhead, 2002.

R.L. Feller (ed.), *Artists' Pigments*, Vol. 1, National Gallery of Art, Washington, USA/OUP, Oxford, 1986.

M. Farnsworth, "Ancient Pigments", *Journal of Chemical Education*, 28 (1951).

Simon Garfield, *Mauve*, Faber & Faber, London, 2000.

Oliver Garnett, *Colour: A Social History*, The National Trust, 2000.

R.J. Gettens & G.L. Stout, *Painting Materials: A Short Encyclopaedia*, reprint of 1942 edition, New York, 1966.

F. Hamilton Jackson, *Mural Painting*, Sands & Co., London, 1904.

R.A. Higgins, "The Polychrome Decoration of Greek Terra-cottas", *Studies in Conservation*, 15 (1970).

Historic Paints Ltd, *A Treatise and General Primer on the Properties of Early American Paints*, Historic Paints Ltd, USA, 1994.

Arthur Seymour Jennings, *Paint and Colour Mixing*, 7th ed., Trade Papers Publishing, London, 1926.

Catherine Lynn, "Colors and other Materials of Historic Wallpapers", *Journal of the American Institute for Conservation*, Vol. 20, No. 2.

Maclehose and Brown, *Vasari on Technique*, Dent 1907, Dover 1960.

Ralph Mayer, *The Artist's Handbook of Materials and Techniques*, 4th ed., Faber & Faber, London, 1981.

Thos. Parsons and Sons Ltd, *Historical Colours*, reprint, Thos Parsons and Sons Ltd, London, 1937.

Michel Pastoureau, *Bleu, Histoire d'une Couleur*, Editions du Seuil, 2000.

Traditional Paint News, *Journal of the Traditional Paint Forum*, 1994.

A. Roy (ed.), *Artists' Pigments*, Vol. 2, National Gallery of Art, Washington, USA/OUP, Oxford, 1992.

Frank S. Walsh, "The Early American Palette: Colonial Paint Colors Revealed", *Paint in America: The Colors of Historic Buildings*, (R.W. Moss ed.), John Wiley & Sons Inc, USA, 1994.

E. West Fitzhugh (ed.), *Artists' Pigments*, Vol. 3, National Gallery of Art, Washington, USA/OUP, Oxford, 1997.

Georgian Group Guide No. 4, *Paint Colour*, 2nd ed., UK, 1991.

classical and early texts on color and pigment

Leon Battista Alberti, *On Painting*, trans. C. Grayson, Penguin, London, 1972 and 1991.

Aristotle, *On the Soul*, book II, vi–viii, book III, i–iii, v, trans. W.S. Hett, Harvard University Press, 2000.

Aristotle, "On Colors" in *Minor Works*, trans. W.S. Hett, Harvard University Press, 2000.

Aristotle, *Parva Naturalia, On Sense and Sensible Objects*, trans. W.S. Hett, Harvard University Press, 2000.

Cennino Cennini, *Il Libro dell'Arte*, ed. F. Brunello, 1971.

Plato, *Timaeus, 36: Colours*, trans. D. Lee, Penguin Classics, 1977.

Pliny the Elder, *Natural History*, (book II 151–3, book IX 125–127, book XXXIII 111, books XXXIV–XXXVII, trans. J.F. Healy, Penguin Classics, London, 1991.

Theophilus, *On Divers Arts*, (1122), trans. Hawthorne and Smith, Dover, New York, 1979.

Translations of the major medieval works such as the manuscripts of Jehan Le Begue and Alcherius can be found in the republished 1849 work by Mary P. Merrifield, *Medieval and Renaissance Treatises on the Art of Painting*, Dover, 1967. (Two volumes bound as one.)

color theory, mapping, and systems

Roy S. Berns, *Billmeyer and Saltzman's Principles of Color Technology*, 3rd ed., John Wiley and Sons Inc., 2000.

Färgrapport F28, *Color Order Systems and Environmental Color Designs*, ed. Anders Hård and Lars Sivik, Scandinavian Color Institute, 1983.

Färgrapport F22, *On Studying Color Combinations*, ed. Anders Hård and Lars Sivik, Scandinavian Color Institute, 1989.

Johann Wolfgang von Goethe, *Theory of Colors*, trans. Eastlake 1840, reprinted M.I.T., 1970.

Wilhelm Ostwald, *The Color Primer*, ed. Faber Birren, English edition, Van Nostrand Reinhold, New York, 1969.

Charles A. Riley, *Color Codes*, University Press of New England, Hanover, USA, 1995.

Paul Zelanski and Mary Pat Fisher, *Color*, 3rd ed., Herbert Press, 1999.

color vision and perception

Edith Anderson Feisner, *Colour*, Laurence King, 2000.

Dennis Baylor, "Colour Mechanisms of the Eye", *Colour Art and Science*, ed. Lamb and Bourriau, Cambridge, 1995.

John Berger, *Ways of Seeing*, Penguin, London, 1972.

B. Berlin and P. Kay, *Basic Color Terms*, University of California Press, 1969.

The Colour Group, *Newsletter*, Colour Group (Great Britain, www.colour.org.uk)

Malcolm Longair, "Light and Colour", *Colour Art and Science*, ed. Lamb and Bourriau, Cambridge, 1995.

John Mollon, "Seeing Colour", *Colour Art and Science*, ed. Lamb and Bourriau, Cambridge, 1995.

H. Varley (ed.), *Colour*, Marshall, London, 1980.

M.D. Vernon, *The Psychology of Perception*, Penguin 1962.

Michael Wilcox, *Blue and Yellow Don't Make Green*, Artways, Australia, 1998.

Ludwig Wittgenstein, *Remarks on Colour*, ed. G.E.M. Anscombe, Blackwell, 1977.

H. Zollinger, *Color, A Multidisciplinary Approach*, VCH, Zurich, 1999.

color and art

D. Bomford and A. Roy, *Colour*, National Gallery Co. Ltd., London, 2000.

N. Charlet, *Yves Klein*, Vilo, Paris, 2000.

John Gage, *Colour and Culture*, Thames and Hudson, London, 1993.

John Gage, *Colour and Meaning*, Thames and Hudson, London, 1999.

Paul Hills, *Venetian Color*, Yale, 1999.

Johannes Itten, *The Art of Colour*, John Wiley and Sons Inc., 1961 and 1973.

Johannes Itten, *The Elements of Color*, Van Nostrand Reinhold, New York, 1970.

Trevor Lamb and Janine Bourriau (eds.), *Colour Art and Science*, Cambridge, 1995.

color and place

Michael Lancaster, *Colorscape*, Academy, 1996.

Michael Lancaster, *Britain in View*, Quiller, 1984.

Jean-Philippe Lenclos, *Les couleurs de l'europe*, Moniteur, 1995.

Hibi Sadao, *The Colours of Japan*, with an introductory essay by Kunio Fukuda, trans. John Bester, Kodansha, Tokyo, 2000.

Hibi Sadao, *Japanese Detail*, with an introductory essay by Kunio Fukuda, Thames and Hudson, London, 1989.

Raghubir Singh, *River of Colour: the India of Raghubir Singh*, Phaidon, London, 1998.

Ed Taverne and Cor Wagenaar (eds.), *The Color of the City*, V+K Publishing, 1992.

Bonnie Young and Donna Karan, *Colours of the Vanishing Tribes*, Booth Clibborn, London, 1998.

contemporary culture and color

David Batchelor, *Chromophobia*, Reaktion, 2000.

Norman Foster, *30 Colors*, V+K Publishing, Blaricum, 1998.

Derek Jarman, *Chroma*, Vintage, London, 1995.

Rem Koolhaas/OMA, Norman Foster, Alessandro Mendini, *Colors*, V+K Publishing/Birkhauser, 2001.

NCS, *Top 300 Colors in Design, Architecture and Manufacturing, 2002–2003*, Scandinavian Color Institute, 2002.

Maggie Toy (ed.), *Color in Architecture*, Architectural Design publication, 1996.

paint suppliers and stockists

paint manufacturers matched to color swatches in this book

Benjamin Moore & Co.
51 Chestnut Ridge Road
Montvale
New Jersey 07645
tel 1-800-344-0400
email info@benjaminmoore.com
www.benjaminmoore.com
On-line order service available for all Benjamin Moore paints and the Color Preview Professional Color Selector. Also offers a color matching service. Visit the website to find your local dealer.

Benjamin Moore New Look Decorating Center
110–1990 South Ogilvie Street
Prince George
British Columbia V2N 1X1
tel (250) 561-1888
fax (250) 562-8225
email newlooksales@newlookdecorating.bc.ca
www.newlookdecorating.bc.ca
On-line order service available for all Benjamin Moore paints and the Color Preview Professional Color Selector. Also offers a color matching service. Visit the website to find your local dealer.

Glidden
tel 1-800-454-3336
www.gliddenpaint.com
Visit the website to find your local dealer.

Pratt & Lambert
tel 1-800-BUY-PRAT
email webmaster@sherwin.com
www.prattandlambert.com
Offers an on-line design service through the Pratt & Lambert Personal Design Center. Visit the website to find your local dealer.

Sherwin Williams Co.
101 Prospect Avenue
Cleveland
Ohio 4415
email webmaster@sherwin.com
www.sherwin-williams.com
Visit the website to find your local dealer.

selected stockists of paints matched to color swatches in this book

The Home Depot
Customer Care Department
2455 Paces Ferry Road
Atlanta
Georgia 30339
tel 1-800-553-3199 (US)
tel 1-800-668-226 (Canada)
www.homedepot.com
Stockists of Glidden paints. Visit the website to find your local dealer.

Janovic
30–35 Thomson Avenue
Long Island City
New York 11101
tel (718) 786-4444
fax (718) 361-7288
email info@janovic.com
www.janovic.com
Stockists of Benjamin Moore and Pratt & Lambert paints. Visit the website to find your local dealer.

Johnson Paint Co. Inc.
355 Newbury Street
Boston
Massachusetts 02115
tel (617) 536-4065
fax (617) 536-8832
email webmaster@johnsonpaint.com
www.johnsonpaint.com
Stockists of Benjamin Moore and Pratt & Lambert paints. Offers on-line and mail order service throughout the US and overseas.

other paint manufacturers offering a color matching service

Cloverdale Paint (US)
570 South Michigan Street
Seattle
Washington 98106
tel (206) 762-9274
fax (206) 762-9312
email seattle@cloverdalepaint.com
www.cloverdalepaint.com
Call the Cloverdale Paint Professional to match a paint to any
wallpaper, fabric, or other color swatch

Cloverdale Paint (Canada)
6950 King George Highway
Surrey
British Columbia V3W 4Z1
tel (604) 596-6261
fax (604) 597-2677
email helpdesk@cloverdalepaint.com
www.cloverdalepaint.com
Call the Cloverdale Paint Professional to match a paint to any
wallpaper, fabric, or other color swatch

General Paint (Canada)
950 Raymur Avenue
Vancouver
British Columbia
tel (604) 253-3131
fax (604) 253-3136
email gpinfo@generalpaint.com
www.generalpaint.com
Call the General Paint Professionals to match a paint to any
wallpaper, fabric, or other color swatch.

other manufacturers of quality paints

Hallman Lindsay Quality Paints
PO Box 109
1717 North Bristol Street
Sun Prairie
Wisconsin 53590
tel (608) 834-8844
fax (608) 837-1064
email paint@hallmanlindsay.com
www.hallmanlindsay.com
Visit the website to find your local store.

McCormick Paints
2355 Lewis Avenue
Rockville
MD 20851
tel (301) 770-3235
fax (301) 770-9814
email info@mccormickpaints.com
www.mccormickpaints.com
Order on-line or visit the website to find your local store.

The Old Fashioned Milk Paint Co. Inc.
436 Main Street
PO Box 222
Groton
Massachusetts 01450-0222
tel (978) 448-6336
fax (978) 448-2754
email sales@milkpaint.com
www.milkpaint.com
Traditional paints made from earth pigments in "Colonial" and
"Shaker" shades. Order by phone or visit the website to find
your local store.

useful color terms

saturation

The degree to which colors are intense on the one hand or grayed, tinted or otherwise sullied on the other. A fully saturated color is one at its most brilliant, pure, and intense, a hue. Defined as chroma divided by lightness.

color memory

The phenomenon whereby we ignore visual stimuli and use a memory of a color to ensure its constancy under varying lighting conditions. A means of ensuring an artificial color constancy.

additive colors

Additive colors are those which, when mixed, produce another color of pure hue but greater luminosity, e.g. the primary colors of light.

subtractive colors

Subtractive colors (e.g. of paint) are those which when mixed, cancel out the reflection of large portions of each other's wavelengths of light, reflecting only those wavelengths which they have in common. Thus a greenish blue mixed with an acid yellow will yield a bright green; a purplish blue mixed with orangeish yellow will produce an olive color. Secondary subtractive colors will therefore always appear darker than predicted.

tint

Example: a tint of blue is a light blue, blue plus white.

shade

Example: a shade of blue is a dark blue, blue plus black.

tone

Example: a tone of blue is a grayed blue, blue plus gray.

cusp color

A new term to describe those complex (often muddy or grayed colors) which appear to change color under different lighting conditions. These are therefore colors which do not conform to the cognitive phenomenon of color memory. Two examples are grayish green-blue and pink made with bluish red oxides. They appear to take on separate chromatic identities when lit with, say, the extremes of warm tungsten lighting (color temperature 2,900* K) and cool bluish light from a densely cloud-covered sky (color temperature 7,000*K). Because of the tendency of bright daylight to veer between the latter and full spectrum direct sunlight, it is complex colors which inhabit the borders of blue and violet that are likely to be cusp colors.

chroma

A reference for the saturation of any hue in relation to an equivalently luminous gray. In other words, the purity or intensity of a color, not its lightness or darkness or its hue. You can alter the chromatic value of colors on your TV by slowly reducing the picture from full color to black and white. The Greek word for color.

hue

The separately identifiable character of a color, e.g. red, orange-red, orange. The tiny steps around the color wheel can be measured by the color's hue and which are determined by a color's wavelength.

value

Lightness (whiteness or blackness) of any color, no matter how weak or grayed.

complementaries

On color models, complementaries sit on opposite sides of the wheel. In theory they are colors that when mixed in the correct quantities will cancel each other out and produce gray or black (pigments) or white (light). In practice, subtractive, pigment complementaries produce murky browns. Complementary colors when placed against each other will play optical tricks and appear to hover and excite each other (red and green for example). The three- and four-color subtractive models (see color models 1 and 2 on pages 8–9) offer different and interesting arrangements of complementaries; the three-color additive model (of light primary and secondary colors) offers an arrangement of complementaries with the best optical properties.

Palette 44
1 BMCC, *457 Icy Morn*
2 BMCP, *OC20 Pale Oak*
3 P&LCC, *1031 Moss Rose*
4 BMCP, *2077-20 Gypsy Pink*
5 BMCC, *1565 Mount Saint Anne*
6 BMCC, *1573 Castle Walls*

Palette 45
1 BMCP, *2001-10 Ruby Red*
2 BMCP, *2048-10*
    Sherwood Forest
3 BMCP, *2015-20 Orange Burst*
4 BMCP, *2052-10 Ocean Topic*
5 BMCC, *007 Pinata*
6 BMCC, *529 Sweet Daphne*

Palette 46
1 BMCP, *2076-30*
    Crushed Berries
2 BMCC, *549 Honey Dew*
3 BMCP, *2004-30*
    Raspberry Pudding
4 BMCP, *2036-40*
    Meadowlands Green
5 BMCP, *2001-20 Bonfire*
6 BMCP, *2049-50 Spectra Blue*

Palette 47
1 BMCC, *199 Barley*
2 P&LCC, *1500 Sherwood Green*
3 BMCP, *2168-10 Fall Harvest*
4 SWCS, *SW 6943 Intense Teal*

Palette 48
1 BMCC, *056 Mountain Agate*
2 BMCP, *2136-10 Black Knight*
3 BMCC, *891 Opal*
4 BMCC, *1663 New Born's Eyes*
5 BMCC, *181 Pan For Gold*

Palette 49
1 BMCP, *2089-20 Rosy Peach*
2 BMCP, *2059-40 Yosemite Blue*
3 BMCP, *2158-40 Golden Mist*
4 BMCP, *2058-50 Aquarium Blue*
5 BMCP, *2120-20 Black Iron*

Palette 50
1 BMCC, *912 Linen White*
2 BMCC, *1081*
    King Arthur's Court
3 BMCC, *1186 Rosestone*
4 P&LCC, *1121 Gentility*
5 BMCC, *907 Evening White*
6 BMCC, *169 Aura*
7 BMCC, *1543 Plymouth Rock*
8 BMCC, *1542 Plymouth Rock*
9 BMCC, *834 Bright and Early*
10 BMCC, *1620 Blue Heather*

11 BMCC, *907 Evening White*
12 BMCC, *173 Happily Ever After*
    or BMCC, *181 Pan For Gold*
13 BMCC, *508 Tree Moss*
14 BMCC, *983 Smokey Taupe* or
    BMCC, *990 Hampshire Taupe*
15 BMCC, *1564 Beach Glass*
16 BMCC, *812 Blueberry Hill*
17 P&LCC, *2062 Café Cubano*
18 BMCC, *110 Starfish*
19 BMCC, *458 Sage Tint*
20 BMCC, *507 Grecian Green*
21 BMCP, *2067-60 Windmill Wings*
22 P&LCC, *1203 Daydream*
23 BMCC, *046 Salmon Mousse* or
    BMCC, *045 Romantica*
24 BMCC, *054 Farmers Market*
25 BMCC, *1196 Burnt Sienna*
26 BMCC, *035 Baked Clay*
27 BMCC, *1566 Stonybrook*
28 BMCC, *444 Cedar Grove*

Palette 51
1 BMCP, *2068-60 Purple Lace*
2 BMCC, *912 Linen White*
3 BMCC, *1262 Paris Romance*
4 BMCP, *2113-10*
    Chocolate Sundae

Palette 52
1 BMCP, *2080-20*
    Confederate Red
2 BMCC, *076 Corlsbad Canyon*
3 P&LCC, *1881 Arabesque*
4 BMCP, *2054-60 Old Pickup Blue*
5 BMCC, *1423 Angels Wings*
6 P&LCC, *2304 Rubidoux*

Palette 53
1 BMCP, *2159-40 Amber Waves*
2 BMCP, *2094-40 Soft Cranberry*
    or BMCP, *2094-50 Desert Rose*
3 BMCC, *1089*
    Chilled Chardonnay
4 BMCP, *2089-30 Pink Minx*
5 BMCC, *816 Aqua Marina*
6 BMCC, *1018 Shabby Chic*
7 BMCC, *HC138 Mill Hill Springs*
8 BMCC, *724 Peacock Feather* or
    BMCC, *723 Spring Rain*
9 BMCC, *824 Yin Yang*
10 BMCP, *2156-20 Pumpkin Blush*
11 BMCC, *1418 Oriental Iris*
12 BMCC, *837 Sheer Romance*
13 BMCC, *1421 Bistro Blue*
14 BMCP, *2115-50 Iced Mauve*
15 BMCP, *2053-40 Blue Lake*
16 BMCP, *2068-20 Grape Gum*

Palette 54
1 P&LCC, *1123 Siberian Iris*
2 BMCP, *2103-10 Natural Brown*
3 BMCP, *2158-30*
    Delightful Golden
4 BMCP, *2091-10 Tea*

Palette 55
1 P&LCC, *405 Shades of Spring*
2 BMCC, *1818 Russet*
3 BMCP, *2069-10 Deep Mulberry*

Palette 56
1 BMCP, *2145-20 Terrapin Green*
2 BMCC, *461 Rose Pine*
3 BMCC, *247*
    Consentino Chardonnay
4 BMCP, *2082-10 Chestnut*

Palette 57
1 BMCP, *2080-10*
    Raspberry Truffle
2 BMCP, *2157-20 Golden Harvest*
3 BMCP, *2015-10 Electric Orange*
4 P&LCC, *1267 Duckling*

Palette 58
1 BMCC, *675 Thunder Bird*
2 BMCC, *1494 Vale Mist*
3 BMCC, *221 Golden Garden*
4 BMCC, *131 Sevilles Oranges*

Palette 59
1 BMCC, *877 Sand Dollar*
2 BMCC, *961 Sea Pearl*
3 BMCC, *675 Thunder Bird*
4 BMCC, *1378 Lazy Afternoon*
5 BMCC, *1655 Northern Green*
6 BMCC, *798 Blue Suede Shoes*
7 BMCC, *564 Gumdrop*
8 BMCC, *776 Santa Monica Blue*
9 BMCC, *320 Manillo*
10 BMCC, *802 Riviera Azure*

Palette 60
1 BMCC, *768 Atlantis Blue*
2 BMCP, *2068-30*
    Scandinavian Blue
3 BMCC, *691 Dartsmouth Green*
4 BMCC, *1251 Mulberry Wine*
5 GCC, *15RB 07/237*
    Windsor Purple
6 BMCC, *704 Del La Mar Blue*
7 BMCC, *792 Mystical Blue*
8 BMCC, *819 Southern Belle*
9 BMCP, *2077-30 Hot Lips*
10 BMCC, *805*
    New York State of Mind
11 BMCC, *829 Sunrise*

12 BMCC, *805*
    New York State of Mind
13 BMCC, *820 Misty Blue*
14 BMCC, *823 Steel Blue*

Palette 61
1 P&LCC, *1073 Secret*
2 BMCP, *2077-30 Hot Lips*
3 SWCS, *SW 6859 Feverish Pink*
4 P&LCC, *1079 Tulip Purple*

Palette 62
1 BMCP, *2022-30 Bright Yellow*
2 BMCP, *2018-30 Citrus Blast*
3 BMCP, *2016-20 Citrus Orange*
4 BMCP, *2014-30 Tangy Orange*
5 BMCP, *2001-10 Ruby Red*
6 BMCP, *2077-30 Hot Lips*
7 SWCS, *SW 6981*
    Passionate Purple
8 BMCP, *2071-30 Mystical Grape*
9 SWCS, *SW 6965 Hyper Blue*
10 GCC, *67BG 19/394*
    Spectrum Blue
11 P&LCC, *1270 Blue Zircon*
12 BMCP, *2044-20 Leprechaun*
13 BMCP, *2033-10 Yellow Green*
14 BMCP, *2031-20 Paradise Green*
15 SWCS, *SW 6920 Center Stage*
16 GCC, *60YY 65/669 Parakeet*

Palette 63
1 BMCC, *586 Northern Lights*
2 BMCP, *2034-30 Grassy Fields*
3 BMCP, *2077-30 Hot Lips*
4 BMCP, *2086-30 Rosy Blush*
5 BMCP, *2086-30 Rosy Blush*
6 BMCP, *2086-40 Deep Carnation*
7 BMCP, *2002-10 Vermilion*
8 BMCP, *2015-10 Electric Orange*
9 BMCP, *2068-30*
    Scandinavian Blue
10 BMCP, *2066-30*
    Big Country Blue

Palette 64
1 P&LCC, *1151 Ethereal* or
    SWCS, *SW 6967 Frank Blue*
2 BMCP, *2079-40*
    Spring Time Bloom
3 BMCP, *2169-10 Racing Orange*
4 BMCP, *2022-30 Bright Yellow*
5 BMCP, *2005-60 Pink Pearl*
6 BMCP, *2014-10 Festive Orange*
7 BMCC, *795 Faded Denim*
8 BMCC, *1268 Cotton Candy*
9 BMCP, *2170-40 Coral Spice*

Palette 19
1 BMCC, *449 Serene Breeze*
2 BMCC, *037 Rose Blush*
3 BMCC, *275 Banana Cream*
4 P&LCC, *1096 Moor*
5 BMCC, *1643 Franklin Lakes*
6 BMCC, *773 Athenian Blue*
7 P&LCC, *1305 Maitland Blue*
8 BMCC, *525 Savannah Shade*
9 BMCC, *067 Del Ray Peach*
10 BMCC, *1475 Graystone*
11 P&LCC, *2132 Old Guard*
12 BMCC, *1566 Stonybrook*
13 BMCC, *043 East Lake Rose*
14 BMCC, *025 Vivid Peach*
15 BMCC, *450 Nob Hill Sage*
16 P&LCC, *1454 Mistletoe*
17 BMCC, *219 Coronado Cream*
18 BMCC, *1468 Willow Creek*
19 BMCC, *HC-127 Fairmont Green*
20 BMCC, *1323 Currant Red*
21 BMCC, *1665 Mozart Blue*
22 BMCC, *1565 Mount Saint Anne*

Palette 20
1 BMCC, *995 Mocha Cream*
2 BMCP, *2028-50 Wales Green*
3 BMCC, *808 Sapphire Ice*
4 BMCC, *618 Robin's Nest*
5 BMCC, *1380*
   Peace and Happiness
6 BMCP, *2073-50*
   Purple Easter Egg
7 BMCC, *1595 Rocky Coast*
8 BMCP, *2116-50 African Violet*
9 BMCC, *1453 Pebble Creek*
10 BMCP, *2013-10*
   Outrageous Orange

Palette 21
1 BMCP, *2023-60 Butter*
2 P&LCC, *1882 Pagoda Red*
3 BMCC, *445 Greenwich Village*
4 BMCP, *2022-30 Bright Yellow*
5 BMCP, *2133-10 Onyx*

Palette 22
1 BMCP, *2133-70 Tundra*
2 P&LCC, *1729 Casava*
3 BMCP, *2145-10 Avocado*
4 BMCC, *1603 Graphite*
5 BMCP, *2125-50*
   Sweet Innocence
6 BMCC, *1261 Paisley Pink*
7 BMCP, *2127-60 Feather Gray*
8 BMCC, *515 Baby Turtle*

Palette 23
1 BMCP, *2076-60 Dog's Ear*
2 BMCP, *2079-50 Rhododendron*
3 P&LCC, *1673 Seaweed*
4 P&LCC, *1875 Faded Rose*
5 BMCP, *2074-20*
   Summer Plum

Palette 24
1 BMCP, *2068-20 Grape Gum*
2 GCC, *68YR 28/701*
   Fiesta Orange
3 BMCP, *2163-40 Metallic Gold*
4 BMCP, *2077-30 Hot Lips*
5 BMCP, *2050-10 Willow Green*

Palette 25
1 BMCC, *315 Oxford Gold*
2 P&LCC, *1763 Zinnia Gold*
3 BMCP, *2015-10 Electric Orange*
4 BMCP, *2011-10 Orange*
5 BMCC, *021 Jupiter Glow*
6 BMCC, *1315 Poppy*
7 BMCP, *2037-10 Amazon Moss*
8 BMCC, *790 Bayberry Blue*

Palette 26
1 BMCC, *827 Lake Placid*
2 BMCP, *2072-40 Wild Orchid*
3 BMCC, *828 Airway*
4 BMCC, *809 Soft Jazz*

Palette 27
1 BMCC, *1472 Silver Chain*
2 BMCC, *1416 Whispering Wind*
3 SWCS, *SW 6239 Upward*
4 BMCC, *1531 Victorian Garden*
5 BMCC, *1411 North Cascades*
6 BMCC, *710 Kensington Green*
7 BMCC, *1620 Blue Heather*
8 BMCC, *682 Warm Springs*

Palette 30
1 BMCC, *1203 Warm Sienna*
2 BMCC, *1613 Silent Night*
3 BMCC, *995 Mocha Cream*
4 BMCC, *996 Ashen Tan*
5 BMCC, *989 Alphano Beige*
6 BMCP, *2019-30 Sunflower*
7 BMCC, *1197 Pumice Stone*
8 BMCP, *2084-10 Brick Red*

Palette 31
1 BMCC, *189 Morgan Hill Gold*
2 BMCC, *191 Macadamia Nut*
3 BMCP, *2156-30 Jack O'Lantern*
4 BMCC, *165 Glowing Apricot*
5 BMCC, *1316 Umbria Red*
6 BMCC, *1255 Pink Panther*
7 BMCC, *034 Spiced Pumpkin*
8 BMCC, *039 Sharon Rose*
9 BMCC, *1274 Warm Earth*
10 BMCC, *1256 Amaryllis*

11 BMCC, *466 Garden Path*
12 BMCC, *472 Aganthus Green*
13 BMCC, *1049*
   Toasted Marshmallow
14 BMCC, *1053 Sierra Hills*
15 BMCP, *2116-30 Cabernet*
16 BMCC, *1446 Dusk to Dawn*
17 P&LCC, *2272 Petaluma*
18 BMCC, *984 Stone Herth*
19 BMCC, *063*
   Pennies from Heaven
20 BMCC, *053 Crazy for You*
21 BMCC, *980 Woodcliff Lake*
22 BMCC, *1473 Gray Huskie*
23 BMCP, *2113-10*
   Chocolate Sundae
24 P&LCC, *2036 Ashford*

Palette 32
1 BMCC, *256 Westwood Tan*
2 BMCC, *1039 Stone House*
3 BMCC, *1066 Barely Beige*
4 BMCC, *445 Greenwich Village*
5 BMCC, *494 Lewiville Green*
6 BMCC, *504 Nature's Reflection*
7 BMCC, *711 Boca Raton Blue*
8 BMCC, *992 Ticonderoga Taupe*

Palette 33
1 BMCC, *203 Fields of Gold*
2 BMCC, *HC-16 Livingston Gold*
3 BMCC, *035 Baked Clay*
4 BMCC, *1259 Beaujolais*
5 BMCC, *735 Deep Sea Green*
6 BMCP, *2135-30 Nocturnal Gray*
7 BMCC, *629 Weeping Willow*
8 BMCC, *1582 Deep River*

Palette 34
1 BMCC, *027 San Antonio Rose*
2 BMCC, *077 Fiery Opal*
3 BMCC, *INT.RM Black*
4 BMCC, *054 Farmer's Market*
5 BMCC, *048 Southwest Pottery*
6 BMCC, *INT.RM Atrium White*

Palette 35
1 BMCC, *INT.RM White*
2 BMCP, *2007-40 Blue Lapis*
3 BMCP, *2171-10 Navajo Red*
4 BMCP, *2066-10 Blue*
5 BMCP, *2059-40 Yosemite Blue*
6 BMCP, *2045-10 Green Bay*
7 BMCC, *444 Cedar Grove*

Palette 36
1 BMCC, *159 Peach Crisp*
2 BMCC, *1250 Magic Potion*
3 BMCC, *1524 Nature's Scenery*
4 BMCC, *187 Goldfinch*

5 BMCC, *718 Ocean City Blue*
6 BMCC, *1081*
   King Arthur's Court
7 BMCC, *1088*
   Home Sweet Home
8 BMCC, *1526 Evening Grove*

Palette 37
1 SWCS, *SW 7001 Ibis White*
2 BMCP, *2173-10 Earthly Russet*
3 BMCC, *997 Baja Dunes*
4 BMCC, *876 Alabaster*
5 BMCC, *1457*
   White Winged Dove
6 BMCC, *012 Coral Reef*
7 BMCC, *1461 Sterling Silver*
8 BMCC, *988 Frosted Toffee*
9 BMCC, *1521 Nature's Essentials*
10 BMCP, *2172-60 Pink Hibiscus*
11 BMCC, *041 Spoonful of Sugar*
12 BMCC, *1019 Dellwood Sand*

Palette 38
1 BMCC, *1655 Blue Bay Marina*
2 BMCC, *717 Paradiso*
3 BMCP, *2110-10 Taupe*
4 BMCC, *1507 April Showers*
5 BMCC, *1579 Greyhound*
6 BMCC, *465 Antique Jade*

Palette 39
1 BMCP, *2012-10 Tawny Day Lily*
2 BMCP, *OC66 Snow White*
3 BMCP, *2119-10 Space Black*
4 BMCP, *2065-40 Utah Sky*

Palette 40
1 BMCP, *2011-10 Orange*
2 BMCP, *2204-20 Chili pepper*
3 BMCP, *2005-10 Red Rock*
4 BMCP, *2022-30 Bright Yellow*

Palette 41
1 BMCC, *124 Orange Appeal*
2 BMCC, *796 Nova Scotia Blue*
3 BMCP, *2119-10 Space Black*

Palette 42
1 BMCP, *2171-30 Adobe Orange*
2 BMCC, *221 Golden Garden*
3 BMCP, *2061-50 Tidal Wave*

Palette 43
1 BMCP, *2002-10 Vermilion*
2 BMCP, *2014-10 Festive Orange*
3 BMCP, *2041-10 Hunter Green*
4 BMCP, *INT.RM White*

Paint Matches

How to buy the color you like

Below is a list of every color in *Choosing Colors* with—in almost every case—a match to a paint color from some of the most respected paint brands in the US: names like Benjamin Moore, Glidden, Pratt & Lambert, and Sherwin-Williams. It couldn't be easier.

Kevin McCloud

Notes to the paint matches

All references to paint manufacturers and their specific paint ranges are abbreviated as follows:

BMCC = Benjamin Moore Classic Colors
BMCP = Benjamin Moore Color Preview
GCC = Glidden Coordinated Collection
P&LCC = Pratt & Lambert Calibrated Colors IV
SWCS = Sherwin-Williams Color Specifier

Color accuracy and the limitations of this book

This volume has been printed in Hexachrome®, an advanced printing process that uses six component colors rather than the conventional four. While Hexachrome® offers over 3,000 controllable colors, there are still some limitations and variations within the printing process. As a result it is impossible to guarantee the fidelity of the colors reproduced.

The paint matches given below have been matched to all the printed swatches in this book using paint manufacturers' color cards. However, neither the author nor the publisher can take responsibilty for any discrepancies in color, no matter how large, between a swatch color in this book and its corresponding specified manufacturers' color.

You are strongly advised to obtain manufacturers' shade cards or buy test pots before making a purchasing decision. In any case, paint from any manufacturer will vary minutely in color. When buying paint, always check the batch numbers on the can and buy from the same batch whenever possible. If it is not possible to buy from the same batch, mix the cans to achieve a uniform color.

Palette 01
1 P&LCC, *1750 Canary Yellow*
2 GCC, *20YY 37/654*
    Golden Marguerites
3 BMCP, *2023-30 Sun Porch*
4 BMCP, *2021-30 Sunshine*
5 GCC, *61YY 89/135 Moonscape*
6 GCC, *56YY 86/241 Lemon Ice*
7 GCC, *70YY 83/075 Vapor*
8 GCC, *25YY 85/108*
    Coconut Milk
9 GCC, *60YY 71/540 Glitzy Gold*
10 GCC, *45YY 67/259 Costa Mesa*
11 GCC, *68YY 86/042 Marble Falls*
12 GCC, *60YY 83/062 White Swan*

Palette 02
1 GCC, *25YY 49/757 Golden Sun*
2 GCC, *23YY 62/816 Royal Gold*
3 BMCP, *2019-10 Mardigras Gold*
4 GCC, *05YY 42/727*
    Marigold Blossom
5 GCC, *10YY 34/700*
    Butterscotch Tempest
6 BMCC, *1046 Sandy Brown*
7 GCC, *45YY 73/519 Yellow Rose*
8 BMCC, *319 Dalila*
9 GCC, *30YY 26/525 Jazzy Sax*
10 GCC, *20YY 69/238 Stucco*
11 GCC, *37YY 78/312 Falling Star*
12 GCC, *17YY 65/420*
    Pale Orange
13 GCC, *10YY 58/295 Light Topaz*
14 BMCC, *HC-5 Weston Flax*
15 GCC, *31YY 81/214 Honeytone*
    or GCC, *46YY 86/166*
    Popcorn White
16 GCC, *29YY 84/067 Vanilla Latté*

Palette 03
1 SWCS, *SW 6886 Invigorate*
2 BMCP, *2016-20 Citrus Orange*
3 GCC, *68YR 28/701*
    Fiesta Orange
4 GCC, *68YR 28/701*
    Fiesta Orange
5 GCC, *60YR 23/650 Sizzle*
6 BMCP, *HC-75 Maryville Brown*
7 P&LCC, *1849 Orange Berry*
8 GCC, *30YR 67/113 Embrace*
9 BMCP, *2168-40 Peachland*
10 BMCP, *HC-52 Ansonia Peach*
11 BMCC, *075 Flamingo Orange*
12 GCC, *50YR 55/201*
    Lotus Blossom
13 BMCC, *068 Succulent Peach*
14 GCC, *70YR 58/091 Zinfandel*
15 GCC, *70YR 56/190*
    Desert Warmth
16 GCC, *30YR 74/045*
    Easy Feeling

Palette 04
1 BMCP, *2014-20 Rumba Orange*
2 BMCP, *2014-30 Tangy Orange*
3 BMCP, *2013-20 Orange Nectar*
4 BMCP, *2172-10 Copper Clay*
5 BMCP, *2168-40 Peachland*
6 BMCP, *2013-10*
    Outrageous Orange
7 BMCP, *2169-10 Racing Orange*
8 BMCC, *1202 Baked Terra Cotta*
9 BMCP, *2170-30 Autumn Cover*
10 BMCC, *1299 Crimson*
11 BMCC, *040 Peaches 'n Cream*
12 BMCC, *019 Salmon Run*
13 BMCC, *003 Pink Paradise*

14 BMCP, *2173-40 Antique Rose*
15 BMCC, *046 Salmon Mousse*
16 BMCC, *017 Phoenix Sand*

Palette 05
1 BMCP, *2002-10 Vermilion*
2 BMCP, *2000-10 Red*
3 BMCP, *2008-20 Claret Rose*
4 BMCP, *2084-10 Brick Red*
5 BMCP, *2009-40 Pink Peach*
6 P&LCC, *1903 Bryce Canyon*
7 BMCP, *2004-30*
    Raspberry Pudding
8 BMCC, *1321 Holly Berry*
9 BMCP, *2000-60*
    Light Chiffon Pink
10 BMCP, *2089-20 Rosy Peach*
11 BMCP, *1305 Bird of Paradise*
12 GCC, *10YR 25/284 Sweetheart*
13 BMCP, *2096-50 Cappuccino*
14 BMCP, *2090-40 Wild Flower*
15 BMCP, *2006-50 Pink Punch*
16 BMCC, *1278 Palermo Rose*

Palette 06
1 SWCS, *SW 6859 Feverish Pink*
2 BMCP, *2079-30 Peony*
3 No near match
4 BMCP, *2084-20 Maple Leaf Red*
5 SWCS, *SW 6580 Cerise*
6 BMCP, *2077-30 Hot Lips*
7 BMCC, *1343 Fuchsine*
8 GCC, *53RR Fiesta Pink*
9 BMCC, *1340 Pink Ribbon*
10 BMCC, *1362 Cranberry Ice* or
    BMCC, *1363 Melrose Pink*
11 BMCC, *1375 Hidden Sanctuary*
    or BMCC, *1376 Angelina*

12 BMCC, *1272 Princess*
13 BMCC, *1345 Bermuda Breeze*
14 BMCC, *1270 Tara*
15 BMCP, *2074-70 Easter Bonnet*
    or BMCC, *1367 Primrose Petals*
16 BMCC, *1374 Orleans Violet*

Palette 07
1 GCC, *93RB 27/376 Rosita*
2 BMCP, *2071-30 Mystical Grape*
3 SWCS, *SW 6983 Fully Purple*
4 GCC, *90RB 11/140 R.S.V.P.*
5 BMCC, *1378 Lazy Afternoon*
6 BMCP, *2073-40 Purple Hyacinth*
7 BMCP, *2071-40*
    Crocus Petal Purple
8 BMCP, *2072-60 Beach Plum*
9 P&LCC, *1082 Rosy Lavender*
10 P&LCC, *1087 Lilac Time*
11 BMCP, *2068-50 Victorian Trim*
12 P&LCC, *2246 Trout*
13 GCC, *90RB 38/098*
    Emily's Dollhouse
14 P&LCC, *1096 Moor*
15 BMCC, *1402 Spring Iris*
16 BMCC, *1380*
    Peace and Happiness

Palette 08
1 SWCS, *SW 6983 Fully Purple*
2 BMCP, *2068-30*
    Scandinavian Blue
3 P&LCC, *1143 Gloxinia*
4 GCC, *70BB 14/202*
    Contentment
5 BMCP, *2070-40 Spring Purple*
6 BMCP, *2068-40 California Lilac*
7 P&LCC, *1142 Anchusa*

8 P&LCC, *1135 Geneva Blue*
9 BMCP, *2068-50 Victorian Trim*
10 BMCC, *1419 Persian Violet*
11 GCC, *54BB 41/237 Versailles*
12 BMCC, *1453 Pebble Creek*
13 BMCC, *1395 Grape Ice* or
   GCC, *10RB 46/132 Giggles*
14 BMCC, *1416 Whispering Wind*
15 BMCP, *2067-70 White Satin*
16 P&LCC, *1121 Gentility*

Palette 09
1 BMCP, *2066-10 Blue*
2 BMCP, *2065-30 Brilliant Blue*
3 BMCP, *2066-20 Evening Blue*
4 SWCS, *SW 6531 Indigo*
5 SWCS, *SW 6963 Sapphire*
6 BMCC, *797 Athens Blue*
7 SWCS, *SW 6958 Dynamic Blue*
8 BMCC, *830 Harlequin Blue*
9 BMCC, *817 Brazilian Blue*
10 BMCC, *818 Watertown*
11 BMCC, *796 Nova Scotia Blue*
12 BMCC, *822 Riviera Azure*
13 BMCC, *799*
   Mediterranean Breeze
14 BMCC, *808 Sapphire Ice*
15 BMCC, *801 Blue Bayou*
16 BMCC, *821 Blue Ice*

Palette 10
1 BMCP, *2059-20*
   Caribbean Azure
2 P&LCC, *1231 Aquamarine*
3 BMCP, *2060-30 Seaport Blue*
4 BMCP, *2059-30 Laguna Blue*
5 P&LCC, *1273 Copenhagen*
6 BMCP, *2064-60 Bluebelle*
7 BMCC, *1669 Saratoga Springs*
   or BMCC, *1656 Aspen Skies*
8 BMCC, *748 Blue Toile* or
   BMCP, *2054-40 Blue Lagoon*
9 P&LCC, *1259 Prudence*
10 BMCC, *1663 New Born's Eyes*
   or BMCP, *2058-50*
   Aquarium Blue
11 BMCC, *1640 Dusky Blue* or
   BMCC, *1641 Blue Porcelain*
12 BMCC, *1656 Aspen Skies* or
   BMCP, *2054-50 Seaside Blue*
13 BMCC, *743 Picture Perfect*
14 BMCP, *2051-70 Crystal Blue*
15 P&LCC, *1265 Sterling Blue*
16 BMCC, *1654 Ashwood Gray*

Palette 11
1 SWCS, *SW 6947 Tempo Teal*
2 P&LCC, *1376 Cavern Pool*
3 BMCP, *2045-20 Lawn Green*
4 BMCP, *2048-20 Juniper*

5 BMCP, *2052-30*
   Tropical Turquoise
6 BMCP, *2045-30, Aruba Blue*
7 BMCP, *2036-30*
   Green With Envy
8 BMCP, *2040-40*
   Summer Basket Green
9 BMCP, *2052-40 Blue Spa*
10 BMCP, *2051-30 Casco Bay*
11 BMCC, *599 Brookdale Gardens*
12 BMCP, *2047-10 Forest Green*
13 BMCP, *2051-40 Majestic Blue*
14 BMCP, *2123-40 Gossamer Blue*
15 BMCC, *633 Appalachian Trail*
16 P&LCC, *1335 Pacific*

Palette 12
1 GCC, *70GY 22/546 Emerald Isle*
2 BMCP, *2030-10 Lizard Green*
3 P&LCC, *1531 Grass Green*
4 SWCS, *SW 6461 Isle of Pines*
5 BMCC, *641 Everglades*
6 BMCC, *586 Northern Lights*
7 BMCC, *573 Four Leaf Clover*
8 BMCC, *1563 Quiet Moments*
9 BMCP, *2040-50 Hazy Blue*
10 BMCC, *572*
   Branch Brook Green
11 BMCC, *688 Seacliff Heights*
12 BMCC, *687 Annapolis Green*
13 BMCP, *2035-50 Spruce Green*
14 BMCC, *638 Pure Essence*
15 BMCC, *694 Colony Green*
16 SWCS, *SW 6192 Costal Plain*

Palette 13
1 BMCP, *2031-20 Paradise Green*
2 BMCP, *2026-10 Lime Green*
3 BMCP, *2027-30 Eccentric Lime*
4 BMCP, *2146-10 Dark Celery*
5 BMCP, *2034-40 Cedar Green*
6 SWCS, *SW 6920 Center Stage*
7 BMCC, *399 Exotic Lime*
8 BMCC, *502 Grasslands*
9 P&LCC, *1496 Apple Green*
10 SWCS, *SW 6443 Relish*
11 BMCC, *478 Sweet Caroline*
12 BMCC, *500 Maidenhair Fern*
13 BMCC, *430 Landscape*
14 BMCC, *540 Country Green*
15 P&LCC, *1654 Misty Green*
16 BMCC, *506 Silver Sage*

Palette 14
1 P&LCC, *2239 Gigs' Grey*
2 BMCP, *HC-169 Coventry Gray*
3 SWCS, *SW 7030 Anew Gray*
4 P&LCC, *2303 Olde Silver*
5 P&LCC, *2241 Carolina Gull*
6 P&LCC, *2318 Lava*

7 BMCP, *HC-87 Ashley Gray*
8 BMCP, *HC-105 Rockport Gray*
9 P&LCC, *2242 Gettysburg*
10 BMCC, *1486 Winterwood*
11 BMCC, *993 Beachcomber*
12 BMCC, *1546 Gargoyle*
13 P&LCC, *2306 Anubis*
14 BMCC, *1488 Sage Mountain*
15 P&LCC, *2039 Cafe Gray*
16 SWCS, *SW 7026 Griffin*

Palette 15
1 GCC, *80YR 13/227*
   Tobacco Road
2 GCC, *70RR 08/150*
   Aberdeen Place
3 BMCP, *HC-51 Audubon Russet*
4 BMCP, *2114-30*
   Desert Shadows
5 P&LCC, *1824 Oakleaf Brown*
6 P&LCC, *1883 Wild Cherry*
7 BMCP, *2110-30 Saddle Soap*
8 BMCC, *HC-74*
   Valley Forge Brown
9 P&LCC, *2083 Oakbuff*
10 BMCP, *2091-10 Tea*
11 BMCC, *HC-73 Plymouth Brown*
12 BMCP, *2095-30*
   Butternut Brown
13 P&LCC, *1818 Russet*
14 BMCP, *2102-10 Earth Brown*
15 BMCP, *2137-10 Otter Brown*
16 BMCP, *2153-10 Golden Bark*

Palette 16
1 BMCC, *1003 Kitten Whiskers*
2 BMCC, *997 Baja Dunes*
3 GCC, *90YR 55/051*
   Kennet Square
4 BMCC, *990 Hampshire Taupe*
5 GCC, *60YR 63/022*
   Notable Neutral
6 BMCC, *1458 Silver Bells*
7 GCC, *60YR 47/034*
   Mandolin String
8 GCC, *60YR 33/047 Hiking Trail*
9 BMCC, *1457*
   White Winged Dove
10 GCC, *90RR 54/018 Disco Ball*
11 GCC, *60YR 47/034*
   Mandolin String
12 GCC, *90RR 33/032*
   Imperial Stone

Palette 17
1 SWCS, *SW 6994 Greenblack*
2–9 All colors based on paints
available from Papers and Paints
Ltd in the UK. Hand-painted swatch
cards and paint in a variety of media

for a full palette of 64 colors can be
bought from Papers and Paints Ltd,
4 Park Walk, London SW10 0AD,
UK or click on www.papers-
paints.co.uk. As noted on page
179, similar colors have been found
in buildings in the US, which have
been researched and documented
by the color analyst Frank S.
Welsh. Full paint samples of the
American colors can be bought
from Frank S. Welsh at PO Box
767, Bryn Mawr, PA 19010, USA.
10 BMCP, *2130-50*
   New Hope Gray
11–39 All colors based on paints
available from Papers and Paints
Ltd in the UK. Hand-painted swatch
cards and paint in a variety of media
for a full palette of 64 colors can be
bought from Papers and Paints Ltd,
4 Park Walk, London SW10 0AD,
UK or click on www.papers-
paints.co.uk. As noted on page
179, similar colors have been found
in buildings in the US, which have
been researched and documented
by the color analyst Frank S.
Welsh. Full paint samples of the
American colors can be bought
from Frank S. Welsh at PO Box
767, Bryn Mawr, PA 19010, USA.
40 Color based on paint tinted with
woad (blue) available from Bleu de
Lectoure, Ancienne Tannerie, Pont-
de-Pile, 32700 Lectoure, France, tel
00 33 (0)5 62 68 78 30; fax 00 33
(0)5 62 68 91 52; email info@bleu-
de-lectoure.com; www.bleu-de-
lectoure.com.

Palette 18
1 BMCC, *833 Evening Sky*
2 BMCP, *2035-10 Seaweed Green*
3 BMCP, *2049-20 Oasis Blue*
4 BMCC, *1593 Adagio*
5 BMCC, *784 Blue Macaw*
6 SWCS, *SW 7069 Iron Ore*
7 BMCC, *735 Deep Sea Green*
8 P&LCC, *1454 Miseltoe*
9 BMCP, *2087-10 Neon Red*
10 P&LCC, *1874 Mineral Red*
11 BMCP, *2085-20 Pottery Red*
12 P&LCC, *2273 Dunswit*
13 BMCC, *1160 Chadwick Brown*
14 BMCC, *262 Golden Hills*
15 BMCC, *214 Valley View*
16 BMCC, *369 Mulholland Yellow*

picture credits

1–2 Edina van der Wyck; 12–13 *Elle Decoration*/Chris Tubbs/designer Laurence Kluft; 16 Red Cover/Huntley Hedworth; 17 above Red Cover/Reto Guntli; 17 below left Graham Atkins Hughes/designer Karim Rashid; 17 below right Verne Fotografie; 20 *Marie Claire Maison*/Marie-Pierre Morel/J. Pascal Billaud; 21 above left Ray Main/Mainstream; 21 above right IPC Syndication/© *Living Etc.*/Chris Dawes; 21 below left Vega MG/Guilio Oriani/architect Betti Sperandeo/Studio'98 (+39 02 86 45 84 97); 21 below right Red Cover/Winfried Heinze/architects Chris & Milla Gough-Willets/ practice Studio Azzurro; 24 above left Guy Bouchet; 24 above right The Interior Archive/Mark Luscombe-Whyte; 24 below Narratives/Jan Baldwin/designed by Cath Kidston; 25 above *Marie Claire Maison*/Marie-Pierre Morel/Marie Kalt/designers Antoine Audiau & Manuel Warosz; 25 below left Verne Fotografie; 25 below right Agence Top/Roland Beaufre; 28 Verne Fotografie; 29 above Red Cover/ David George; 29 below left Ray Main/Mainstream/designer Philippe Starck; 29 below right Verne Fotografie; 32 Paul Massey; 33 above left Alexander van Berge; 33 above right IPC Syndication/© *Homes & Gardens*/Debi Treloar; 33 below *Marie Claire Maison*/Vincent Leroux/Catherine Ardouin; 36 above left Ray Main/Mainstream; 36 above right Deidi von Schaewen/architect Eli Mouyal; 36 below left Minh + Wass; 36 below right The Interior Archive/Simon Upton; 37 *World of Interiors*/Eric Morin/designer Agnès Emery; 39 above Narratives/Jan Baldwin/designed by Rita Konig; 39 below left Red Cover/Polly Farquarhson; 39 below right The Interior Archive/Edina van der Wyck/designer Sophie Hicks; 41 above Red Cover/Andreas von Einsiedel; 41 below left Taverne Fotografie Agency/John Dummer/Karin Draaijer; 41 below right Red Cover/© *Maison Côté Sud*/Bernard Touillon/architect Paul Anouilh; 43 above left IPC Syndication/© *Ideal Home*/Claudia Dulak; 43 above right Ray Main/Mainstream/architect Patrick Gwynne; 43 below The Interior Archive/Simon Upton/reproduced by kind permission of the National Trust (Carlyle's House); 45 above Vega MG/Eugeni Pons/José Tarrago (+34 968 150 255); 45 below left Red Cover/Reto Guntli; 45 below right Vega MG/Giorgio Possenti/architect Vincent van Duysen; 46–47 *World of Interiors*/Bill Batten; 48 The Interior Archive/Fritz von der Schulenburg; 51 Ken Adlard; 54 Arcaid/Richard Bryant/Homewood House Museum, the Johns Hopkins University, Baltimore, Maryland, USA; 55 Ken Adlard; 58 Ken Adlard; 59 National Trust Photographic Library/ Geoffrey Frosh; 61 *World of Interiors*/Bill Batten; 62–63 National Trust Photographic Library/Eric Crichton; 64 The Interior Archive/Edina van der Wyck; 67 Sanoma Syndication/Peter Kooijman; 68–69 The Interior Archive/

Mark Luscombe-Whyte; 71 The Interior Archive/Edina van der Wyck/designer Jenny Armit; 73 Camera Press/© *Visi*/Designers Guild; 74–75 Red Cover/© *Maison Française*/Francis Amiand/designer Florence Baudoux/LUMA (+33 1 45 49 37 12); 76 Minh + Wass; 78–79 *Marie Claire Maison*/Ingalill Snitt/P. Bailhache; 80 The Interior Archive/Fritz von der Schulenburg; 83 Narratives/Jan Baldwin/designer Lena Proudlock (+44 1666 500 051); 84 Andrew Wood/Rupert & Caroline Spira; 86 Ray Main/Mainstream/20th Century Design; 88 Agence Top/ André Chadefaux; 91 The Interior Archive/Edina van der Wyck/architect John Lautner; 92 Ray Main/Mainstream; 94 *Vogue Living*/Mikkel Vang/Christine Rudolph; 97 World of Interiors/Bill Batten; 99 Ray Main/Mainstream/designer Paul Daly; 101 *World of Interiors*/James Mortimer; 102–103 Arcaid/Richard Bryant/architects Tsao & McKown; 107 Narratives/Jan Baldwin/designer Alastair Hendy; 108–109 *World of Interiors*/Bill Batten; 111 Tim Street-Porter; 112 Narratives/Jan Baldwin/ MMM Architects (+44 20 7286 9499); 114–115 Red Cover/Ken Hayden/ designer Jonathan Reed; 116 Sanoma Syndication/Hotze Eisma; 119 Andreas von Einsiedel/designer David Carter; 121 Robert Montgomery & Partners/Pia Tryde; 122 Chris Tubbs/designer Oswald Boateng; 125 Les Publications Condé Nast/© *Architectural Digest*/ Vincent Thibert; 126 Arcaid/Richard Bryant/architect Carl Larsson; 128 Guy Obijn/architect Jo Crepain; 131 Ricardo Labougle/Hotel Boquitas Pintades, Buenos Aires; 132–133 *World of Interiors*/Bernard Touillon; 134 The Interior Archive/Edina van der Wyck; 135 Craig Fraser/ architect Bert Pepler; 138–139 Camera Press/© *Visi*/Adriaan Oosthuizen; 140 Geoff Lung/designer Tim Janenko Panaeff; 143 Minh + Wass/construction Tyler Hays; 144 Gilles de Chabaneix; 145 *Marie Claire Maison*/Marie-Pierre Morel/Daniel Rozensztroch; 146 Andrew Wood/Rupert & Caroline Spira; 149 The Interior Archive/ Luke White/architect David Mikhail; 150–151 The Interior Archive/Ianthe Ruthven; 153 Red Cover/Ken Hayden/architect Lord Richard Rogers/designer Jonathan Reed; 154–155 IPC/© *Homes & Gardens*/Winfried Heinze/Philip Hooper at Cibyl Colefax & John Fowler; 157 Minh + Wass; 158 Vega MG/Gianni Basso/designer and owner Giuseppe Sala; 162 Ray Main/Mainstream; 163 Andreas von Einsiedel/designer David Collins; 164–165 Taverne Fotografie Agency/Hotze Eisma/Hanne Lise Poli; 166 *Elle Decoration*/Chris Tubbs/architect Stuart Church; 170 *Marie Claire Maison*/Dan Tobin Smith/David Souffan; 171 The Interior Archive/Edina van der Wyck/architect Lord Richard Rogers; 172 Red Cover/© *Maison Française*/Barbel Miebach; 174 *World of Interiors*/Eric Morin.

acknowledgments

There are a number of individuals who I wish to thank for their involvement with this book, without whose help it would have appeared a rather pathetic volume. Jane Turnbull deserves mention for her guidance and advice, Lisa Pendreigh and Helen Lewis for their patient editing and design, Nadine Bazar for extensive picture research, Sarah Howarth for her support and research, Laura Baer and Polly and Henry Reeve for color research and matching, and Anne Anderson for encouraging me to paint. Also thanks to Jane Duncan of the Color Group, Ole Cornelissen of Cornelissens, Dr Andrew Middleton of the British Museum for research material, Colin Mitchell Rose of Craig and Rose Paints, and Mike and Lula Gibson for collecting bits of wall from India.

I want to especially thank Patrick Baty for his support and for providing research material, Keith Edwards for spending time pigment matching and pointing me in new directions, and Anne Furniss—whose idea this book was—for her vision.

Several institutions and companies have been enormously helpful in providing research material and source subject matter, some wittingly, others not. Some are large museums, others are small facilities, run on small budgets and dependent upon the energy of a few passionate individuals. It would be an injustice not to list them, so thanks to:
National Geological Survey; Design Museum, London; Victoria and Albert Museum, London; British Museum, London; Papers and Paints Ltd, London; Haynes Motor Museum, Sparkford; The National Motor Museum, Beaulieu; Volkswagen, Milton Keynes; The American Museum in Britain, Bath; Humbrol Paints, Natural Color System (UK); Craig and Rose Paints; SAS Regimental Association; The Color Library at the Royal College of Art, London; Michael Harding, artists' colorman; National Art Library; Drawings Collection at the Royal Institute of British Architects, London; Geological Collection at The Natural History Museum, London; British Standards Institute Library; Potterton Books; Spectrocam, The Color Group; Traditional Paint Forum; Oil and Color Chemists Association.

Thanks also to the paint manufacturers—Benjamin Moore & Co., Glidden, Pratt & Lambert, and Sherwin Williams Co.—who kindly supplied their catalogs for the paint matching.

I must also thank my colleagues at work for their tolerance and particularly Christopher Hoare for his support. Finally, I would never find the time to research, color-match, or write were it not for the unfailing support and friendship of my wife and the long-suffering patience of my children.

For Hugo, Grace, Milo, and Elsie who are blessed with young eyes.